CLICK HAPPY

YOUR GUIDE TO A MEANINGFUL LIFE & CAREER IN
THE DIGITAL ERA

MOLLY PITTMAN

Hardcover ISBN: 978-1-7347-4545-0

Paperback ISBN: 978-1-7347-4540-5

E-book ISBN: 978-1-7347-4541-2

This book was produced with Laura Gale. For more information about producing a book about your business, go to www.lauraiswriting.com.

CONTENTS

To my students, this book is for you.
To Laura Gale, this book wouldn't have happened without you!
May we all find a life that "clicks".

FOREWORD: EZRA FIRESTONE

The book you are reading right now could change your life. It's designed to help you make the transition from wherever you are at this moment into a successful, thriving career in digital marketing. If you're burned out, bored, or you just know in your heart that it's time for a change, this book is for you.

No matter who you are or where you're from, the opportunities created by the Internet are unrivalled — and they are only getting bigger. A lot of people think they've missed the boat with digital marketing and working online, but in reality, digital commerce is only just beginning to take off. We are still at the onset of this revolution. There is an opportunity for you in this space, and this book is going to help you find it.

You might not believe me, but I would know. I barely made it out of high school, and yet I am a living Internet success story.

Growing up in an intentional community — a commune in California — we had an abundance of love but an alarming lack of actual resources. The water would turn off, the power would go out... we were broke. Today, it's one of the most successful intentional communities in the US, still going strong today after 50 years, but when I was a kid, money was the one thing we hadn't yet figured out.

So it might not come as a big surprise that I didn't go to college. When I left high school I moved to New York City to play poker, because at the time it was the best option I had for making money. A few years later, I realized I wasn't going to generate the kind of wealth I wanted with poker, and fell into e-commerce by chance around 2005.

When I got started, I was not rich, I was not well-educated, and I didn't know anybody doing what I wanted to do. But today I am the CEO of a seven-figure company, an eight-figure company, and I founded the seven-figure company Molly now runs!

What's special about this book is that it shows that no matter where you're starting, there's a place for you in the digital economy. It doesn't matter if you're a waitress or a lawyer or a stay-home parent or you grew up on a commune.

You don't need a fancy degree or even experience working online. There is an opportunity afoot if you are willing to give it your attention, and no one is a better example of that than Molly herself.

When I first met Molly Pittman, she was a junior intern in someone else's company, fresh out of bartending, helping to run a launch for one of my information products. That was seven years ago. Today she's a world-famous leader in the digital marketing community and the go-to authority on paid amplification for Internet business owners.

I couldn't have told you back then that one day I would be writing the foreword to her book, but I'm not surprised. Not at all.

I'm very selective about who I follow and endorse, but I'm thrilled to be able to support Molly. When I decide whether

I'm going to follow an influencer, consume their content, hire them as a service provider, and recommend them to people, I want to know if they have integrity. I ask myself if I can trust them, if they are actually doing what they're teaching, and if they have any proof that what they're teaching is successful for their students.

For a lot of people, the answer to those questions is no. A lot of people are teaching stuff they did a long time ago. They're no longer actively practicing what they preach, and their students are not getting the results they want and deserve.

And then on the other end of the spectrum, there's Molly! There's nobody better in our industry at teaching how to be successful at paid advertising and digital marketing. She has the track record to prove it. She has the '10,000 hours' to prove it. She has the raving fan base of successful students, and the lifestyle to prove it too.

What I value most about Molly's work is the amount of care, attention and enthusiasm she brings to it. In our industry, there are a lot of incredibly smart people, but very few who truly love what they're doing, and have figured out how to teach it. Molly has a very high emotional intelligence. It is innate to her; she understands people. She understands how to make her message resonate. She's a born teacher and a natural leader.

To be fair, since I've known her so long and clearly think she's amazing, I'm not an objective source on Molly.

The objective proof is in the results she has empowered other people to create. I have close to a million people following me — business owners and e-commerce specialists who can smell bullshit a mile away — and they love what they've learned from her. They love her energy and enthusiasm and that she has empowered them to achieve results in their business above and beyond their hopes and dreams.

People come away from her teaching believing they can do what she does, feeling confident that they are going to get it right.

We need teachers like Molly right now, because our industry has a problem. That problem is the culture of hustle, grind, and sacrifice that so many entrepreneurial leaders are pushing.

You've heard it all: *Do whatever it takes to win. Sleep when you're dead. If you're not growing, you're dying.*

Many people don't even realize this is a problem. They believe it's just the price of success. But those same people burn out and leave a trail of chaos in their wake. The hustle leaves no time for your personal life, no time for your relationships, no time for your hobbies. You don't take care of your body or your mental health. And ultimately, something's gotta give: either your business suffers because you never take a break and burn out, or the rest of your life burns down because you refuse to prioritize anything over your work.

Parkinson's Law says that work will expand to fill the time that you give it. This has never been more true than it is right now, while digital is solidifying as one of the most powerful economic environments in the world. Digital follows you everywhere. You work from your computer. You find your clients and sell your products online. You have constant access to the Internet. And if you're not careful, the digital space becomes your whole existence.

The push-hard, win-at-all-costs mentality just doesn't serve us anymore. It's not necessary, it's not effective, and it's just not a fun way to live. The better approach is holistic and adaptive, where work can be *one* of your priorities, not your *only* priority. It's not a zero-sum game anymore, where you either win or you lose everything.

You're allowed to have balance, and Molly is a great

example of someone who has come through that burnout culture. She knows how compelling it is to throw every last bit of your energy into your work, because you think more work equates to more success.

But success is a marathon and not a sprint. Success is about consistency: showing up every day with a good attitude and taking the next step forward, while keeping a container around the energy you give to the work. Managing your energy matters — we are still at the very beginning of this wave of digital commerce, and if you're going to ride the wave for years to come, you need sustainable strategies to keep you engaged and effective.

I cannot recommend this enthusiastic, vibrant, powerful woman highly enough. She's a leader in this industry who does the work, teaches it, and shares the opportunities freely. I hope you'll take Molly's lessons to heart, and start to create those magical moments in your own life and career when everything just *clicks*.

— Ezra Firestone.

INTRODUCTION

In 2013, I moved to Austin as a bartender from Lexington, Kentucky. Just a few years later, I was managing millions of dollars in ad spend and leading a team of industry experts. My journey into digital changed my life completely, and I want to show you how you can create the same change in your own life.

And since any transformative experience is also bound to bring up some challenges along the way, I also want to share some personal stories to help you avoid some of the problems I faced.

I am a survivor of burnout. By 2015, I was working 16 hours a day. I was obsessive about my job, stressing constantly about this campaign or that. I wasn't spending time with anyone outside my industry, and even though I was constantly on the edge of crashing, I felt incredibly lucky to have landed a job at DigitalMarketer, one of the biggest players in the digital space. I thought that working as hard as I possibly could was the only way to prove my commitment.

While I was young enough to get away with all that for a

while, after several years of all-out hustle, my health was a mess and I felt terrible. I was anxious, exhausted and extremely stressed. My pilot light had burned out.

This book is about how all that changed, and how everything can change for you too.

———

My time at DigitalMarketer wasn't the first time my life had been upended.

During high school, I played soccer competitively, and was planning to go to a Division One school in order to play professionally. I loved soccer, and it was the most important thing in my life. It taught me a lot about being part of a team, and about the capabilities of our minds and bodies.

But when I was 16, I tore my ACL (a crucial ligament in the knee). No matter how much rehab I did, I was never as good as I was before the injury, and in the following year I had two ankle injuries. By the last game of my final school year, I knew I was done. It was a huge lesson that even if you are excellent at something, you still might not get the outcome you want and expect. It made me realize that I really wanted to build a skillset that could not be taken away from me.

Once soccer was off the table, my heart really went to travel. My grandmother took me to Italy on vacation towards the end of high school, and I loved it. As a result, I ended up going to a small liberal arts school in Lexington called Transylvania University to study marketing and business — secretly my big motivation for choosing Transy was that they had a program where I could study abroad for the same amount as my tuition, so all my scholarships went towards that.

I have never been so nervous in my whole life as I was in the weeks leading up to my study-abroad program in Rome. I didn't know anybody from outside Kentucky, and going to Rome taught me a huge amount of empathy. It helped me understand *why* people are different from me, and why surrounding yourself with all kinds of people is so powerful.

When it came time to graduate college, my advisor, Dr. Poynter, who taught my class on entrepreneurship, suggested I move to Austin, Texas. She had recently been there for a conference, and saw that there was a lot of tech, a lot of young people, and a lot of growth in multiple industries. I had been thinking that I would go into marketing for a craft beer or spirits company, so I went to visit Austin, renowned for its bar scene. I moved a few months later with $2000, no job, and no plan.

I got a bartending job when I arrived and a few weeks later, I found an ad that might have been the most impactful thing ever advertised on Craigslist. It was written by Perry Belcher and it went something like this:

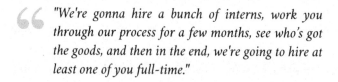

> *"We're gonna hire a bunch of interns, work you through our process for a few months, see who's got the goods, and then in the end, we're going to hire at least one of you full-time."*

That seemed like a fun game to me, and I figured I might get a full-time job at the end of it. I didn't even own a computer at the time, but I applied and landed one of the internships. The leadership split us up into teams and gave us some business ideas to develop. They wanted to see who could work well together, who was a good public speaker, who could do research, who could strategize effectively and so on.

At the end of the internship, I was hired full-time, and I went to work directly with Ryan, working on organic social media. After a few months, my first Traffic & Conversion Summit came around. I knew Ryan was famous online, but I was not prepared for what I saw. I discovered there were thousands of people who wanted this information so badly that they would travel from all over the country just to come to hear him speak.

But that was when the power of digital really clicked for me. I knew I wanted to learn more, and I asked Ryan if I could start buying Facebook ads. The media buyer had just left, so he said yes. He gave me a few courses, and made me promise to use the knowledge for good... not for anything unethical. He was very careful to make me understand that media buyers can get any message out into the world, and so we need to make sure they are messages that have a positive impact — a rule that has underpinned everything I've done ever since. Ryan gave me a $1000 to spend on Ezra Firestone's 'Brown Box Formula' training, and the only rule was that I had to bring back more money than I spent.

No pressure, right?

Well, I made $3000 with that first campaign, and from there I was just hooked. I loved it. Media buying was a skill I was completely fascinated with, and I was all in. I was getting great validation from my boss and my peers, I loved the industry, and I felt like I had found my place. A year later, I was presenting on stage at Traffic & Conversion Summit... a professional leap that I could never have imagined, and that I'll tell you're about in Chapter Two.

I fell in love with teaching, and people started saying things like, "Molly, that tip that you gave changed my business." Or, "I was able to send my daughter to college because of what you taught me about Facebook ads." I'm so grateful to Ryan for pushing me towards this — I would not have done it on my own, but now I can't imagine doing anything else.

From there, I started running webinars, and built my first product for the Native Ad Academy. By 2014, DigitalMarketer was really growing. My skill set had broadened, but there had also been some issues within the company, and I had gone to Ryan to try to solve them. So when he was ready to hand off more of the leadership, he knew I could handle challenging situations, and I was made VP of Marketing for the whole company.

That was a huge year. With the promotion came responsibility for all paid media, email marketing, funnels, and marketing operations. I also started the Perpetual Traffic Podcast with Ralph Burns and Keith Krance in 2015. The idea for the podcast came up organically during a conversation, and while it meant even more on my plate, it felt like a great opportunity (and at the time of writing this book, we had passed 4 million downloads, which is an amazing feeling).

I wanted to be good at my job. In fact, I wanted to be the best. And not only to be the best, but to make it look easy too.

Looking back, it was a perfect storm of overwhelm brewing.

Between all my responsibilities, managing my team and delivering the podcast, I ended up working 16-hour days, staying at the office all night, working as hard as I could to show my commitment. I didn't have the tools to balance all these huge new responsibilities and to maintain a sense of healthy balance for myself.

There are times when that hustle and intensity is valuable, but it's not sustainable. As time went on, I really started to burn out. In 2015 I went through a lot of tough personal stuff, including a breakup, and a big conflict with a close family member that caused a lot of stress. I really wasn't taking care of myself — I would work 12 hours at the office, go home, eat some takeout, open a bottle of wine and work for another three hours.

There was always something else to learn, something else to make, something else to optimize. I still wanted to prove that I was the best, so I could easily justify sleeping three hours a night and never spending any time on stuff outside of work.

I kept growing and doing better in my work, but I was tired and sick, and completely out of balance. I finally admitted to myself that things weren't working, and in 2016 I started working with a nutritionist, and learned some strategies to control my schedule a bit more.

As my energy returned and I had the brain space to actually think strategically, and to pay attention to my own needs, I realized that I was spending 70% of my day doing stuff I didn't love. Things were changing a lot at DigitalMarketer as we continued to grow, and I started feeling boxed in by my role.

In 2017 I went to Colorado for a week for my birthday, and one day went for a really long hike on my own. Out in nature, where it was so quiet and beautiful, something clicked again, and I knew it was time for me to move on. I knew there was a path forward for me where I could live a more balanced life, which would allow me to help more people.

As soon as I came back, I called Ryan to tell him. It was probably the hardest thing I've done in my life so far. It was like leaving a family, but also leaving my identity — who would I be on the other side of this? I didn't know how I would make money, or what people would think of me, but at this point, I knew that I had built great relationships with my colleagues and my students, and had proved how much I cared about this industry.

It was time to do something bold, and in the next two years, I started an online business, chose a few key clients to work with. By 2020 I was CEO of one of the most successful internet marketing companies in the world.

———

On average we sleep eight hours a day, work eight hours a day, and have the other eight hours for our personal life.

That means we spend half our waking hours working and half of them on "life". Unfortunately, most of us are out of balance, prioritizing work at the cost of our personal growth and happiness.

I wanted to represent both sides of our lives in this book, and to show that both sides can work in harmony — that you don't have to sacrifice one side to win at the other.

The first three chapters after this introduction share my personal journey and all the important lessons I've learned along the way. From Chapter Four — 'The Story of Digital' — we'll jump into the strategies and tactics that will help you to become a better marketer. Enjoy both, as they are both necessary in a balanced life!

Of course, if you want to jump right into the nuts and bolts of becoming a media buyer, feel free to skip the first three chapters and get straight into Chapter Four.

No matter what you choose, this book is designed to help you make the transition from wherever you are right now into a fulfilling and flexible career in digital marketing. No matter where you're starting from, there's a role for you in digital, and as you read *Click Happy*, you're going to learn the fundamentals of marketing and the key elements of working in digital.

This means that no matter what you do, you'll have a deep understanding of what makes digital marketing work, how all the different roles interact, and what goes into creating successful, sustainable marketing campaigns across all the available channels. Armed with this knowledge, you will become very valuable to any business you choose to work in — whether you join an established team or strike out on your own.

The focus from Chapter Four onwards will largely be on media buying, because that's what I know best (and I think it's where the biggest opportunities lie for personal and professional growth), but we'll also cover the other roles available in this space.

I've included interviews with good friends (who also happen to be experts in their respective fields) from many other key roles in digital marketing at the end of this book, so that you can get a clear sense of which path will be right for you. This book is tailored towards a few specific people:

- You've spent some time in corporate, you have experience in marketing and working with teams, but you're not happy. You're lacking autonomy, you're restricted by red tape, and you spend most of your time doing stuff you don't care about. You're always 'on' and answering to somebody. Even when you have a weekend or vacation, you have a lingering anxiety that someone might need you, and you can never completely disconnect.
- You own a business and you're frustrated by a lack of growth. You've done all the hard things that are necessary to start a business, but you're having trouble finding a reliable traffic source. You know your business could be growing a lot faster, but you don't have the knowledge or bandwidth to run

ads yourself. You know it would make a huge difference to have someone in-house helping you out with paid ads, but you don't know how to hire for the role, and you have so many questions: how much do you pay a media buyer? What should they be doing each day? How long should it take them to get good at this? Should they be incentivized by ad spend or by revenue? Should you hire an agency or bring this in house?

- You're in digital marketing already, and you want to get better at your craft. You want to be invaluable to your company or clients. Maybe you're ready to go out on your own, but you don't know how to start a business or agency — you need to understand the different models available in this space, as well as the risks and rewards involved in starting your own business, running your own schedule, and overseeing campaigns from a strategic leadership position.

- You're in college, looking into the future and realizing that the traditional path might be going away soon. You're familiar and comfortable with technology, and understand how online platforms work, because you grew up with them. You want a career that's fun and fulfilling, and lets you work on your own terms. You know that you won't be taught these skills in college, even if you're doing a business or marketing degree, because the landscape just changes too fast, and you want to set yourself up to be successful right out of the gate.

Marketing, at its core, really comes down to connecting with other humans and understanding them. If you have a mental block about your work, or if you're not in a good place with your health or mentality, it becomes very hard to be empathetic or understanding towards other people. If you want to be good at marketing or buying media, you really have to be the best version of yourself, and we're going to talk a lot about how to do that throughout this book.

We've all been taught that the person who works the hardest wins. And working hard is important, especially when you're starting out. But ultimately, the success you have in this field is not only about how many hours you work: the results of your work are even more important.

When your campaigns bring in more money than you spent on them, you prove your value to the business. As you get more experienced, you can apply your skills to each part of the customer journey, and gradually help the business improve its revenue and profit at every stage of that relationship. No one can argue with that kind of value, so your success is not reliant on the number of hours worked or the number of meetings you go to or whatever political power games you can win.

Digital marketing is both an art and a science. The science part is easy — you test ideas, track the numbers, and apply the results. But the part that's an art requires creativity.

To be creative, you have to give yourself time and space. You need to have balance in your life, where you take care of your body through nutrition and exercise, and taking time to travel or spend time with people you care about.

You need time away from work to process ideas and information in order to be creative, and so you need to be comfortable stepping away from your computer regularly to be good at this.

Some of my best ideas for marketing campaigns happen when I'm on vacation or talking with cool people, because my brain is in a completely relaxed and making new connections. For a lot of people, the idea of working less in order to do the work well is completely counterintuitive. But I know from experience it works.

I'm so excited for you to start down this transformative path, creating a life that is meaningful, fulfilled and successful— where what you want and need *click* into place for you. To do that, you need to know where this industry has come from, and where we're going, so let's get started.

FINDING MY VALUE

It was 2010, the summer between my sophomore and junior year in college and I was back in my hometown of Danville, KY, for summer break.

I was 19 and I'd had quite a few jobs in my lengthy career thus far. I'd worked for a photographer, at a deli, front desk at a gym, and a few other odd jobs. I thought I'd already figured out how this "job" thing worked and was excited for any chance to trade my time for money to spend on booze, snacks, and gas for my 1998 Chevy Blazer (HA!).

At the time I assumed that the rest of my career would follow suit... trading my time for money. I would move up the career ladder, and that would mean that my time would be worth even more money. Ah, the dream!

This was the plan, and I stuck to it for the next seven years until I left my last job at DigitalMarketer in 2017 (more on that to come).

Part of the plan for that summer was to find a job. Mom let me know that there was a new restaurant opening on Main Street. They would serve brick oven pizza and craft beer. Nothing like this existed in Danville, KY in 2010. Pizza

AND beer? A potentially lucrative job at a social "hot spot" in this small town? This was a big deal! 19-year-old Molly wanted in on the action.

The next morning I walked into the new restaurant, handed over my resume, explained I had experience in hospitality and was hired on the spot. Because I wasn't old enough to serve alcohol yet, my first job was as a hostess making minimum wage — no tips. I was happy nonetheless. It was more money than I would have had without a job, I loved my co-workers, and was engulfed in the excitement of experiencing the launch of a new business.

I had no idea that the seemingly simple experience of working at a pizza restaurant would prepare me for so much more to come.

The first Friday night of the very first weekend that we're open, the Great American Brass Band Festival is in full swing and Danville is at full capacity.

The restaurant was completely full for the first time. We had a line out the door and down the block. The owners were first time restaurateurs, and we were not prepared for this! We didn't even have a cash register yet — the business was run on pencil and paper — and I had certainly never been a restaurant hostess before.

At this moment I had a choice. I could cave to the pressure of hangry families barking about wait times and pizza toppings and tell my boss that it was too much, that they had thrown me in the deep end with the sharks and no life boat, and they could find another, more qualified hostess.

Or I could rise to the occasion, solve problems, think for myself, be a self-starter and just throw myself in.

By 7pm that evening I'd figured out a system that would allow us to estimate the wait time. That meant we could call people when their table was ready to decrease congestion at the front door, and I could sell pizza by the slice to the customers waiting for their tables.

The evening was deemed a huge success. I got my first bonus on that first night of work. From there, I took every opportunity to help the business grow, even if it was outside of my job responsibilities. Because of that, I worked my way up the ladder quickly. That summer I became a server, bartender, and then assistant manager. I was making as much money as I would've expected in a post-college job and I was enjoying every second of it.

"Destruction is essential to construction. If we want to build the new, we must be willing to let the old burn... but at first it's very scary. Because once we feel, know, and dare to imagine more for ourselves, we cannot unfeel, unknow, or unimagine. There is no going back. We are launched into the abyss -- the space between the not-true-enough life we're living and the truer one that exists only inside us."
— Glennon Doyle, *Untamed.*

I couldn't stand it any longer.

"Dad, I'm moving to Austin, TX after graduation and I'm sorry. I love you."

Big exhale. Tears. He understood, but it hurt.

The first few months of 2012 were plagued with anxiety. I was due to graduate from university in May, was spending most of my time in bars, and I had no idea what was next... but my next career move wasn't the root of my anxiety.

I felt trapped by my environment, like a bird in a cage.

At the age of 12, I had the opportunity to take a school trip with my grandmother to Italy. That early exposure led to a love of travel, Europe, and adventure that occupied most of my daydreams as a teenager.

For my junior year of college in 2011, I studied at The American University of Rome. I had chosen to study at Transylvania University just so I could be part of this specific study abroad program.

This longing to explore, wander, and experience other ways of life is what drives me. That longing is a steady pulse, deep down in my gut. It's what makes me a great marketer. It's why I've been able to live a life I could never have imagined.

But it hasn't always been the most comfortable path.

I'm the only member of my extended family that lives outside of the state of Kentucky. At home, people don't often "just up and move" and leave their families without a darn good reason. At home, the most common response I get when discussing international travel is about being "safe over there."

During the spring of 2012 I had a meeting with my advisor at Transy, Dr. Julia Poynter (love you Dr. P!), and I told her I had no idea what I wanted to do next with my life. She smirked, reminding me that everyone goes through transitions.

But then she had an 'a-ha!' moment, and a look of enthusiasm appeared on her face.

"Molly, I just got back from a conference in Austin... You need to move there. Just go there. The career opportunities are endless and the city fits you."

After I confirmed that yes, Austin was in the state of Texas, I got that same feeling in my gut that I'd experienced in the registrar's office when I was approved to study in

Rome. The same feeling I had on that first trip with my grandmother.

I recognized this feeling and knew what it meant. I had to go. I couldn't deny myself this adventure.

But suddenly I felt incredibly anxious.

What about my family? My friends? What would they think?

This was much more permanent than studying abroad. I couldn't promise that I would ever come back. I didn't even have a job lined up to explain why I was going!

Sure, there was some fear of the unknown associated with moving to a new place, but I'd already done a test run when studying in Rome. I knew I could leave and survive on my own.

But the anxiety was coming from how this decision, to choose my freedom and to follow my instincts, would affect the people closest to me.

How would they respond?

Would they feel like I thought I was better than them, because I was moving away?

Would they think I didn't love my home because I wanted to live elsewhere?

I felt like a black sheep for wanting something so different to everybody I knew. So, for a few months I waffled back and forth.

Should I stay or should I go?

It wasn't until my roommate at the time, Julia Jarvis, had that same gut feeling and decided to move with me that I felt able to make it real.

Telling my dad was the next step in moving towards this freedom I desired so much.

And guess what?

My dad, mom, my family, my friends… they couldn't have been more supportive of my decision. They celebrated me and sent me off to Austin, into the unknown. They've continued to support me in every step of the journey, and for that I'm eternally grateful.

This wasn't the last time I would step into an unknown place.

Every time I step into the unknown, I experience pain, anxiety, and fear.

Every time I step into the unknown I come out the other side with a more beautiful life than I had before.

Evolution comes at a price. It works the same for all of us. Whenever you feel alone in your fear, remember that this is the human experience. Whenever you feel alone in your anxiety, remember that social media is not an accurate depiction of reality. Nothing is wrong with you — you're just seeing the good stuff everyone else wants to highlight, even though everyone else also experiences some form of darkness.

I actually get excited nowadays when I feel the fear of stepping into the unknown — I know I'm planting the seed for a beautiful outcome that will soon bloom. Trust in that. It will come. Don't let the fear stop you. Don't let it tell you to play small.

Every big "win" I've had came with a lead-up of doubt and fear. Every single one.

This is the dichotomy of life. Good exists with bad. Life with death. Happy with sad. Rest with work. This balance shows up in every facet of your life. Embrace it and you'll live easier.

And as you know by now, I did end up moving to Austin.

This is where I found my true passion and calling in digital marketing. I wouldn't have come across that Craigslist ad if I stayed in my comfort zone in Kentucky. That opportunity just wouldn't have been there.

I got to the place I knew I needed to be for the next phase of my life to commence.

It wasn't easy but it was worth it.

HERE'S WHAT I LEARNED...

1. You determine your value. You may not determine where you start (and I acknowledge my privilege there), but YOU are responsible for where you are going and where you end up. Your dream career isn't just going to appear in front of you — you will have to get uncomfortable and do the work first.

The reason I was able to accelerate at the restaurant was because I made the decision to be as valuable to that business as possible. The more value you bring to the business you're working in, the more leverage you have when it comes to making more money or gaining more freedom. I took this same approach in my roles at DigitalMarketer and even in growing my own businesses.

2. The currency isn't always money. You may be thinking, "No way! If it's not in my job description and I'm not getting paid for it, I'm not doing it".

I can't tell you how many times I've heard this from peers. This is a short sighted way of thinking that will keep you stuck. Dollars aren't the only measurement of growth, especially in the beginning. The more value you bring, the more responsibilities you will get. And the more experience you get, the more money you will make. Don't try to skip ahead!

I ended up making good money at the pizza restaurant, but the greatest value I got from that job were the lessons I'm sharing with you here in this chapter. They shaped my life and the next ten years of my career. If you're only measuring the success of your career by the amount of money you make, you may be missing a valuable lesson that could actually lead you to your next step.

For me I look at whether I'm gaining joy, experiences, lessons, relationships, personal development, professional development, knowledge, and more. That's where the real growth happens. The currency isn't always money, folks.

3. You are not your career. I was just as happy in 2010 working at a pizza restaurant as I am now in 2020 running a multi-million dollar company. That's definitely NOT the dream we're sold in today's society, so how is that possible?

It's because I'm able to separate myself from what I do for work.

Yes, I show up as my genuine and authentic self in my work, but I also know that business is there to support my life. Not to *be* my life. As most of you know, business fluctuates. I've had friends who tie their identity to their work and when business is down, they are down. Don't make this mistake.

Derive happiness and purpose from other areas of life, too. You are so much more than what you do for work, and we'll talk more about this later.

4. Trust and follow your intuition. That "gut feeling" deep in your core is your intuition. It's there to guide you. Listen to it. We experience anxiety and sadness partly because we start to ignore our intuition and prioritize the desires and expectations of other people over our own.

I know it's tough — sometimes it means going against centuries of patterns and beliefs, or feeling like you're letting others down. But stay true to your path. Use your gut as a compass when making decisions on where you live, who you spend time with, what you do for work and so on. This will lead to fulfillment and peace.

5. Your environment matters. I'm a firm believer in doing the most with what you have. That said, I've found that environment has been one of the most important variables to my success. There are places on earth where I simply feel my best when I'm there, and therefore can do my best work and feel the happiest. For me, this is a combination of the energy and dynamics of the people in that community, access to nature, healthy food, travel, like-minded marketers, and more.

This is why I moved from Kentucky to Austin, then to Telluride, Colorado and why I now live in Amsterdam. I wanted to test the impact of our environment as on us as marketers and entrepreneurs, and I can tell you it's huge. Not everyone has the desire to live in other places, but if you do, don't hesitate... it will make a world of difference. Keep in mind that you can always move back, too. Location independence is one of the biggest benefits of this line of work!

6. Make your decisions. For the longest time I didn't trust my intuition and I cared too much about what others think of me. Because of this, I relied mostly on external input when making important decisions. This sometimes led to making decisions that didn't truly resonate with me. While it's great to get feedback from people you trust, and who live a life that you'd want to live, make sure that the decisions you make (especially the important ones) are yours and yours alone.

2

OUT THERE DOIN' IT...

Ahh, now the part of the journey that we usually try to skip… me included!

The phase where you take action.

The "implementation phase" is the MOST important when you're first getting started. Nowadays, it's always running in the background of my life, but early in my career, from 2012 to 2015, implementation is where I lived.

This phase is when you actually go out and *do* the thing. You take action. Create momentum. You're "out there DOIN' it," as we like to say at Smart Marketer.

My first night at the pizza restaurant, I was out there DOIN' it!

When I decided to follow my intuition to Austin, I was out there DOIN' it!

When I asked Ryan to give me a shot at Facebook ads, I was out there DOIN' it!

But sometimes, I have to admit, I haven't been so great at this.

If you find yourself struggling to take action, like I have, first check in on your current emotional state and thought patterns. You may find that you're stuck in a state of fear and anxiety (as we talked about in the last chapter) that's preventing you from taking action or creating stories of doubt as to why you can't do it. Once I identify these and debunk them, I'm usually free to move forward.

For example, I battled an immense amount of negative thoughts and stories in the past year trying to get this book done.

"Who are you to write a book?"

"People will call you out and leave bad reviews."

"You aren't a writer!"

This is called imposter syndrome and we'll discuss it more in depth in a later chapter.

Suffice it to say, I was the queen procrastinator on this project... and not just by a few days or weeks. We're talking almost a YEAR!

(Laura Gale, who helped me write this book — www.lauraiswriting.com — is a damn saint. She pulled this book out of me and willed it to exist. Look her up!)

In hindsight, I don't think I was emotionally ready or had processed enough of my "stuff" to allow me to be as vulnerable as I am here in these stories, and to make this book what it is.

I'm happy we're finally here but I wish I would've done it sooner, to help you all sooner!

So, yes, you gotta get out there and DOOOO it!

But...

Understand that you can not operate 100% in implementation mode, and that you're going to have to deal with your own fears and emotions to really make it work.

And remember that implementation is NOT about becoming a member of the hustle and grind club! Pushing yourself too hard leads to burn out. When I let myself get to the place of burn out, I was *not* out there DOIN' it!

To me, true success and fulfillment comes when you find a balance. That's why we created a free course for YOU, called Balanced Being. You can find it at www. mollypittman.com/clickhappy.

Sometimes we struggle with getting started, sometimes we struggle with turning it off, sometimes we waffle between the two. It's normal. There's no 'right way'. The only wrong way, if you want to have a meaningful life and career, is to do nothing. You've just gotta show up and do it.

In 2012 I was a part-time intern making $12 an hour, by 2015 I had a cushy six-figure salary, an apartment over-looking Austin, and was speaking on stages across the world. These results were in direct correlation to the output and implementation I mentioned earlier (and from joining Digital Marketer at an opportune time).

I can definitely my rocketing success during those years to my dedication to implementation. You've got to be dedi-cated to "doin' it" even when it's really, really hard.

Here's why.

In early February of 2014 Ryan Deiss asked me to come to his office. He explained that he was giving a keynote at DigitalMarketer's annual event, Traffic & Conversion Summit, about native advertising. That's exactly what I was working on at the time, and he asked if I'd be willing to create the presentation for him, since I had the most current experience with native advertising.

I was thrilled to share what I'd learned, and I slaved over the presentation for days.

It was the first marketing education slide deck I'd ever built (who knew that would become my life!), and I handed it over to Ryan a few days before we were all heading to San Diego for the event.

He asked me to present the slides live to him, so that he knew exactly what to say. I did so with great enthusiasm, trying to hide my nerves, in front of my audience of one.

I had no idea at the time, but about four days later, 23-year old Molly would be presenting this exact deck in front of an audience of over a thousand marketers.

When I presented the deck in his office, Ryan decided I could present the information just as well as he could. He wanted to give me a shot at public speaking, and told me it would be me up there instead of him.

With just a few days to prepare, I felt like I was going to puke and pass out all at the same time. I mean... how do you become the keynote speaker at a premiere marketing even with *no* public speaking experience?!

I was honored, but it was the most anxious I've ever felt. I wanted to run, but I knew it was an incredible opportunity, and because I was willing to feel vulnerable and nervous, it was one of the most rewarding experiences of my life. Ryan agreed to sit on stage beside me during the presentation in case I completely froze. Luckily, it rocked!

Not only did I conquer my fear and anxiety, I also found a true passion and gift that has helped me build the life and career that I have now... public speaking. Speaking is truly my art and it feels so good to deliver a transformation to a room of humans who are eager to connect.

There's nothing more fulfilling than discovering your purpose and gifts, especially if you're able to seamlessly fit them into your career and life. We talk more about finding your purpose in our free course Balanced Being (found at www.mollypittman.com/clickhappy).

Thank you, Ryan, for helping me find my gift. I'm grateful that I took action on the opportunity, even though it was hard.

That's where the goodness is, ya'll!

Sometimes we hit bumps in the road. Accepting and learning how to deal with detours is key to a meaningful life. You don't decide when they show up and unfortunately they don't care whether you're busy or not.

In 2015, I was soaring high in my career, as I alluded to in the last chapter. What I didn't tell you is that although my career was at an all time high, the rest of my life was a hot mess.

Three years into my time at DigitalMarketer, I was starting to feel the effects of a life solely focused on work. Although my life looked perfect from the outside, I felt like I was slowly dying on the inside.

I'd lost that feeling of joy and adventure that brought me to Austin. My relationships were suffering. My mind was filled with negative thoughts about myself.

I wasn't taking care of my body.

Scratch that. I was destroying my body.

My diet looked like a few bags of office snacks a day (mostly Cheez-Its) and a TON of coffee. I drank alcohol almost every day, I was exhausted, and I hardly moved my body.

We talk more about taking care of your physical health and how I came out of this in our free course Balanced Being (found at www.mollypittman.com/clickhappy).

I was absolutely *crushing it*, as the cool kids would say, and inside I felt horrible.

To top it off, I had a hell of a year in my personal life. In the beginning of 2015 I went through a painful and significant break up, and later in the year a similarly devastating situation arose in my family.

These experiences shook me to my core and caused me to

turn inward and start asking some scary questions... who am I? How am I treating myself? What role did I play in these experiences, and how can I grow from them?

I'm not sure if this year was the universe telling me to WAKE UP and take care of myself — that there was more to life than work — or some sort of bad luck. Either way, it was an experience very close to what some people call rock bottom, and I'm grateful for the wake up call. It led me to the work I do now, and as a reminder that there's always light on the other side of the hard stuff, a new mentor came into my life too.

In 2015 I was feeling so dark and sad that I Googled "how to be happier."

That's a problem you can solve with a simple Google search, right?

Well, one of the first sites I found was www.gabbybernstein.com. The homepage of her website said "Become the Happiest Person You Know."

I got that feeling again in the pit of my stomach again. My intuition was speaking up: *Yes, Molly, continue scrolling her site, please!*

Gabby Bernstein is a world renowned spiritual leader, multiple *New York Times* bestseller, and named by Oprah as a "new thought leader for the next generation". She's a big deal, but more importantly she is the *real* deal. She's genuine, speaks the truth, and is here to make the world a better place.

A few weeks later, I had read almost every blog post on Gabby's website, watched every YouTube video, and consumed her books. I searched for help and I found it from Gabby. Her content brought me so much clarity and hope that I realised I would eventually make it out of the dark hole I had found myself in.

There was a common theme throughout her material

encouraging us to turn inward for healing and guidance, instead of trying to "fix" everything that was happening externally.

I followed that direction, starting cleaning up my life, making my wellbeing my top priority, and life started coming back together again.

By early 2016, I was starting to feel more like myself, and my work that year was much more productive and impactful. That was the reflection of the personal work I had done the year before and continued to do.

I mentioned to my friend Ralph Burns that Gabby's information had made all the difference. He looked surprised and told me that he knew her — she was actually his client.

Ralph passed my story back to Gabby and to my surprise, she asked to set up a call to meet and give one another advice. I helped her with a live event funnel and was so excited to have met her.

A few years later, right after I left DigitalMarketer, Gabby sent me an email to say the funnel had worked wonders, and asking if I was able to do some consulting. I was thrilled, and we booked a two-day consulting session at her home. We've worked together in various forms ever since.

This just showed me that your gifts can take you all kinds of interesting places if you're willing to just dive in and say yes to things. I have the opportunity to work with a mentor and build a friendship with someone I respect and admire, all because I gave her 60 minutes five years ago and said yes to the opportunity that presented itself.

Gabby was a huge influence on this book, and while it can be scary for a small-town Kentucky girl to work with someone as well-known and influential as Gabby, I always end up feeling fulfilled, peaceful, and happy in my work, my personal life and my inner self. I feel like a balanced being!

(For more on this topic check out our free course Balanced Being, at www.mollypittman.com/clickhappy)

HERE'S WHAT I LEARNED...

1. Do the (hard) stuff. I know you read this in a lot of personal development books and on Instagram but I'm not quite sure how else to say it. Don't try to avoid things that are hard, optimize your life for joy and love always, but don't try to avoid negative emotions. They are part of being human. On the other side is light and a beautiful outcome. But mostly, just LIVE and actually do stuff. Take the leap. Take the trip. Apply for the job. Have the conversation. #outtheredoinit

2. Say yes. It's important to have filters and guiding boundaries in your life that help you decide what you do and don't do, who you spend your time with, what you spend your time on, etc. But, make sure that you're not too closed off to saying yes to opportunities, ESPECIALLY in the beginning of your career. Know that the opportunities won't always show up the way you had imagined or planned. I never in a million years imagined myself as a public speaker. Because I didn't have that image of myself, I could easily have said no to Ryan because it was scary and didn't fit my plan, and I wouldn't have found this gift so early in life. Be open and if it feels good, say yes and give it a shot... even if it's hard.

3. Embrace how connected your work and personal life really are. We treat ourselves as two different people. One version of Molly goes to work, and one version of Molly has a personal life with friends and family. Although it's important to have healthy boundaries, it's impossible to separate these two categories of your life completely because you are ONE, whole individual. Not two different people.

As I discussed above, when I was dealing with personal issues in 2015, that also showed up in my work. When I bounced back in 2016 and started doing the personal work, my career started to gain momentum again. Both parts of your life are deeply intertwined and will be as long as you're still working.

Keep boundaries between them when possible but also give yourself grace if you find one bleeding into the other. We are all human!

4. Help is on the way — just ask. A mistake I've made in the past is thinking that asking for help makes me weak, stupid, or unworthy. It's actually the opposite. Asking for help when you need it is a sign of strength and something that most successful people I know do really well.

In 2015, when I was at rock bottom, I turned to Google to ask for help and ended up sitting in Gabby Bernstein's living room a few years later with all the help I could ever need. If you're struggling, ask for help and follow the opportunities that present themselves.

Don't let your ego get in the way of you receiving the help and support you deserve.

5. Spirituality doesn't have to be religious. When you look at those pie charts that depict all the areas of our lives, spirituality is always a category. For years I felt empty when I'd see that category… "Hmmm. I've got most of them covered but not this one." That's until I met Gabby and realized that I could be spiritual, and have faith and hope, without subscribing to religious beliefs that had never quite resonated with me.

If you don't already have faith in something that matters to you, open yourself up in this category of life, and start looking for the spiritual practice that's right for you. If you're searching for clarity, like I was, check out Gabby's website at gabbybernstein.com

3

BUILDING A NEW REALITY

By 2017, that familiar feeling was back in my gut. That feeling from 2012, the one that brought me to Austin. To DigitalMarketer. To my gifts. To my purpose. To this dream career that had taken off like a rocket ship.

Yup, it was back and more uncomfortable than ever before. Not only was it back, but it was telling me something I was not ready to hear.

I first noticed this feeling when daydreaming about the mountains and recent trips I'd taken to Colorado. This would lead to thoughts of traveling the world. Building my own business. Being free, and living life on my own terms.

I was 26 years old, more experienced, and I understood that I couldn't ignore my gut like I had for months in 2012.

But I did anyway.

I spent the first half of 2017 in a constant battle (and I truly mean *battle*) with myself about leaving my role at DigitalMarketer.

The conversation was too uncomfortable for me to take action immediately, or at least I thought so at the time.

From the outside, my career looked perfect but I had that

feeling again like I was slowly suffocating on the inside. I wasn't being true to myself, but...

How could I WANT to give up this VP of Marketing position that I've worked so hard for?

DigitalMarketer is my family, my tribe, my place... how could I leave this company?

Would I be able to make it on my own?

Who would I be in my career without them?

Will I lose all of these relationships?

Will people hate me? Will they think I'm dumb for leaving?

The fear went on and on. But even though I danced with anxiety and doubt for months, I couldn't shake the fact that it was time for me to move on with my career.

This job had given me so much but was now draining my joy. People around me were starting to notice and as I mentioned in the last chapter, it bled between both my personal and work lives.

August rolled around and I headed off for a week-long road trip through Colorado for my 27th birthday.

I felt more alive than I had all year on that trip. It sealed the deal and reaffirmed that although I was fearful and had doubts, I had to set myself free.

There was more for me to do out in this world and I couldn't do it if I was tied down to a desk in Austin, Texas.

I texted Ryan and ask him to talk. We hopped on a call and through sniffles and then uncontrollable tears, I tried to explain the reality of the situation.

"I'm sorry, I need to leave this job. I'm not happy. I want more freedom. I'm sorry."

He knew it was coming before I'd even called him. He sensed it. This time comes for everyone and Ryan was not blind to that reality.

Although this was one of the hardest decisions of my

short life so far, it was one of the best, and has led me to a new phase in my journey as an entrepreneur.

It's given me a taste of freedom that I never knew existed.

It reaffirmed my faith that on the other side of the really hard stuff (like calling Ryan), there is a lot of hope, happiness, and freedom.

I'm not sure why we call it "going out on our own" when we start a business of our own, The past three years have been a lot less lonely than the phrase makes it sound!

As I reflect on the few years that have passed since I left DigitalMarketer, one theme rings true.

I wasn't starting from scratch.

My skills and experiences stayed with me.

Most of my relationships stayed with me.

And that knowledge, deep down, that gut feeling? That's definitely still with me!

Keep this in mind during transitions in your life. You're never starting from scratch.

Whatever you're currently experiencing is preparing you for your next step, which looks different for all of us.

Don't compare yours to mine.

Be grateful and try to enjoy it, instead of speeding on to the next step.

As you know, I've experienced a few more transitions since the pivotal moment of deciding to go out on my own.

I moved to Colorado and fulfilled my dream of living in the mountains. I healed. I slept. I rested. I became whole in every area of my life again.

Working with clients on my own, I realized that once your career meets your basic needs, something shifts. Once you're financially stable, you start to look at the work you do in a different way. You start to think more about how it feels and the impact you are (or aren't) making.

In 2020, I became a partner and CEO of a marketing education company that feels like home, www.smartmarketer.com. I get to work with my friends and truly serve the world with our skills.

For me, I realized that the reason I feel so at home and satisfied at Smart Marketer is that my values really align with this company and the people that I'm working with.

Our tagline is "Serve the World Unselfishly and Profit"... and that's exactly what we do.

We believe in people over profits.

There are so many businesses where profit is prioritized over people, and I can't tell you how much better this new version feels to me.

Why? Because my personal values and career are in harmony. And that is the goal. It's where the sweet stuff is, ya'll.

As you've already learned, the future of the digital economy is brighter than I think we can comprehend sometimes.

Remember that slow is actually fast, and that there's room for every one of us to have a seat at this table.

And there's room not just for all of us to have fulfilling careers, but to live a life of true meaning and balance. This is what I hope for you, and what we'll be digging into for the rest of this book. It's not too late, and I am here to help you!

HERE'S WHAT I LEARNED...

1. You get to take your skills with you. One of my greatest fears when deciding to leave DigitalMarketer was that I would lose everything that I'd done for five years and essentially would be starting over. My co-worker and friend Russ

Henneberry reminded me that no one could ever take my skills or the experiences I've had in my career away from me. This was comforting, and he was right.

When you leave a job or walk away from the project, you may feel empty handed at first but remember you always have your skill set and the experiences you've had to help you in whatever is next.

2. Transitions are hard but change is inevitable. I wasn't going to work at DigitalMarketer the rest of my life. I knew that deep down, but my loyalty made that reality foggy for a while.

The most successful people I know are very proficient at handling change. It's an inevitable fact of all areas of our life and if you're able to get comfortable in the uncomfortable and to look at transitions as fun and exciting, they'll be a lot easier for you.

3. Relationships will come and go. This one is tough for me. I love people. People are why I'm here, and why I do what I do. When I work with people, I love them like family.

My co-workers at DigitalMarketer *were* my family. I was worried that that would go away when I left. But with most people, nothing changed. Those relationships continued forward and actually aided me in a lot of the success I've had since leaving. But it's not all rosy. I have lost some close friends over drama related to this change. But overall, it wasn't as scary as I'd first assumed, and in the end, I had to make the choice that was right for me.

4

THE STORY OF DIGITAL

In just a few decades, the Internet has completely transformed how we do business, make purchases, spend our leisure time and interact with other people. Digital marketing is one of the fastest-growing fields in business today, and it's becoming so important because the Internet is now the medium where people are purchasing the most stuff, and where they're spending the most time.

A lot of the economy — both nationally and globally — is being driven by what's happening online. Data collected and analyzed by Statista showed that, "in 2017, an estimated 1.66 billion people worldwide purchase goods online. During the same year, global e-retail sales amounted to 2.3 trillion U.S. dollars and projections show a growth of up to 4.48 trillion U.S. dollars by 2021."[1]

In early 2019, Shopify released a collection of statistics and trends mapping the growth of global e-commerce predicting that during the period between 2014 and 2021, we would see an increase of over 275% in worldwide e-commerce sales.[2]

Imagine a mall where everyone for miles around wants to

shop, because that's where all the best stuff is sold. If you have something to sell — a product or service you want to sell to consumers — you would want to have a location in that mall, because that's where all of the foot traffic is. The Internet is that mall. Every day, more and more consumers show up there, and businesses and marketers must follow suit to survive and thrive. We've got to go where they are, and we've got to hang out where they're hanging out.

It's hard to overstate the value of marketing in this huge mall where everyone is spending their time. Media buyers play a critical role in maximizing the impact and efficacy of that marketing, which in turn, makes media buyers incredibly valuable.

The Internet is also changing how we view our place in the world and the opportunities we have to grow and evolve in our professional and personal lives. In 2018, Pew Research published a wide-ranging study called 'The Future of Well-Being in a Tech-Saturated World.'[3] The study canvassed experts from multiple disciplines, and found a wide range of positive impacts that technology is having on our lives:

- Connection: Digital life links us to people, knowledge, education and entertainment anywhere at any time in an affordable, nearly frictionless manner.
- Commerce, government and society: Digital life revolutionizes civic, business, consumer and personal logistics, opening up a world of opportunity and options.
- Crucial intelligence: Digital life is essential to tapping into an ever-widening array of health, safety, and science resources, tools and services in real time.
- Contentment: Digital life empowers people to

improve, advance or reinvent their lives, allowing them to self-actualize, meet soul mates and make a difference in the world.

- Continuation toward quality: Emerging tools will continue to expand the quality and focus of digital life; the big-picture results will continue to be a plus overall for humanity.

With all these powerful changes, we have more opportunities than ever to choose the life we really want for ourselves. We're getting away from the model that you have to go to college to have a range of professional prospects. Even though college can still be really valuable, it's just not required anymore. You don't have to spend several years studying, and getting into lots of debt, just to be able to compete in today's job market. In fact, many of the case studies later in this book include people who don't have a college degree, or who studied something completely different to what they now do professionally.

They say knowledge is power, and life online has given us access to all of humanity's collected knowledge — which means you have a lot of power. You can use that power to change your life, and that's what this book is all about. It's about adding to your knowledge of what's possible, and all the ways that you can work online, to build more autonomy, fulfillment and freedom into your life.

I invited Ryan Deiss, founder and CEO of DigitalMarketer (and one of the early leaders in the digital marketing revolution), to talk about the history of this industry, as well as where he thinks it's going in the future. In the following excerpt from that conversation, he shares insights he has built up over more than 20 years of experience in growing businesses in dozens of niches, all using digital marketing. Ryan is one of the most iconic people in this space, and he has a lot to share when it comes to educating people about online marketing:

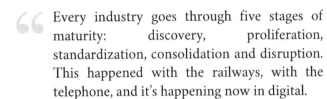 Every industry goes through five stages of maturity: discovery, proliferation, standardization, consolidation and disruption. This happened with the railways, with the telephone, and it's happening now in digital.

The start of this whole trend of marketing online kicked off all the way back in 1994. That was phase one: discovery. The world wide web — the basis of the Internet we know today — was created at CERN in 1989.[4] 1994 is when digital marketing got started, when the very first banner ad got its very first click. The discovery phase of digital marketing lasted until 2000.

I made my very first sale online in 1999, and when I told people I was marketing online, they would assume I was a spammer. The idea of online marketing being legitimate just didn't exist until around 2000 — everyone thought that if you were selling online, you were probably a little bit shady. That changed in 2000, when Google AdWords launched. It was the first self-serve ad platform, and it legitimized digital marketing for the first time.

From 2001, we entered phase two, proliferation, and this lasted up until 2009. All the big-name platforms we know now launched in this period — the very first mommy blog launched in 2002, WordPress launched in 2003, and Facebook, YouTube and Twitter all launched between 2004 and 2006.

The iPhone launched in 2007, so this was when mobile became important, and Facebook's advertising platform was launched in the same year. The proliferation stage is when the gold rush happens and it becomes a bit like the wild west. It was really crazy during this time — you basically just had to show up. It was easy to look really smart, because you were early, but this was more about being in the right place at the right time than about having any particular skill.

By 2009 we were entering the third phase, standardization. This stage is important, because when you have the wild west, you also have snake oil salesmen. Google introduced a quality score to their ad platform in 2009, and more standardization happened on the organic side with the Panda update, which was designed to check the quality of website content. Those two measures got rid of all the scammy advertisers. Then in 2013, Gmail introduced a promotions tab to start filtering out promotional content from people's inboxes, and Facebook started introducing their own 'slap and ban' measures in 2014.

The industry really started to self-regulate between 2009 and 2014, which meant that this was the hardest time to become a digital marketer. A lot of the people who started with me went away at this stage, because they couldn't adapt their methodologies. Molly started her career with us right in the midst of this, and I realized we were never going to win an arms race against Facebook and Google, so from the very start of her training, we played by all the rules.

2015 to 2019 was the fourth phase, consolidation. This was a difficult stage unless you already had a strong brand, because the giants like Facebook, Google and Amazon absolutely dominated global ad share. If you have a strong brand, you can really benefit from the consolidation phase, because people want to sign up with companies that are already thriving and proven. If you don't learn to play by the rules during the standardization phase, you're not going to survive in the consolidation phase.

We entered into phase five, disruption, in 2019. The technology cycle can go one of two places: either the incumbents disrupt themselves and innovate, or they get disrupted by a newcomer who's looking to knock them off the top spot. Clayton Christensen refers to this as the innovator's dilemma — innovating gets you to the top, but once you get there, all you want to do is maintain the status quo.[5] At this stage, to keep moving forward as an industry, we have to try new things and innovate, even when things are working.

The reason I say that the disruption phase started in 2019 is that it was the first year that digital ad sales surpassed traditional offline ad sales. An article published in Adweek in February of 2019 said that "total U.S. ad spend will hit $238.82 billion, with the amount spent on digital media buys surpassing that of traditional and accounting for 54.2 percent of the market. The research shows that digital ad spend will hit $129.34 billion in 2019, while traditional media buys will generate $109.48 billion, with total online media buys generating $172.29 billion in revenue by 2021".[6]

The challenge for most businesses these days is to build marketing teams that can scale with that growth in digital media buying. The days of having one lone marketer who can do everything are gone. The focus has to shift to building better marketing teams. You can't outsource all your marketing to one person, because marketing now directs the entire customer journey, and it takes a team to manage that effectively.

Digital marketing generally breaks down into three groups: acquisition, monetization and operations. Acquisition is made up of organic and paid — you have to have both parts: content is a must, or you'll have nothing to run ads to, and if you're not running ads, you're not going to get enough traction with your content to generate revenue. Monetization is then responsible for actually generating the revenue from the leads and traffic that come in through content and paid ads. Then the operations team is going to build all the technology you need — sales funnels, automations, CRM workflows and so on. These are really advanced systems now and you need specialists.

Eventually you can break each of those roles down into more niche areas — for example search, social, etc under the content role. But if you start with content, paid traffic, promotion and retention, that covers every stage of the customer journey. Building a team that is aligned with the customer journey means that every customer is far more likely to become successful, which creates a virtuous cycle within your business.

Marketers need to think about where they will work best in helping people through their customer journey. Which part of that can you really own? They need to understand all aspects of the customer journey and to recognize how each of the parts fit together, but they really need to go deep on one thing.

I loved what Ryan had to say here: that aligning yourself with a key part of the customer journey is the best way to find your place in digital marketing, and in this book, we're going to delve deep into the customer journey *and* all the parts that need to fit together to create a thriving marketing team.

You'll get a deep understanding of what goes into making effective marketing campaigns, and you'll learn all about the different roles and how they fit together. By the end of this book, you'll know what each role does, why each role matters, how each role interacts, and which one would be best for you. We're going to focus on developing a strategic understanding of digital marketing. We're not going to worry so much about the tactical, button-clicking parts — that all changes way too fast and it's better to join a community like Train My Traffic Person or Team Traffic to stay up to date on that stuff (head to mollypittman.com/clickhappy to access those and many other resources). The purpose of this book is to teach you the fundamentals.

No matter what kind of business you work with, and no matter what role you step into, you will understand how to connect with your audience, and to create marketing that resonates with them and moves them to action. You'll understand your place in this world, and find the ways to work that make you thrive.

5

A NEW WAY TO WORK

Marketing is about connecting with people, and the key to success in this field is to serve your audience selflessly. In digital marketing it is so easy to lose sight of the human element, because we all get so caught up in the tactical stuff. People get stuck thinking about why a particular ad set isn't converting like they had predicted, or whether they should be using this or that targeting tool, but they're missing the point — often their strategies aren't working because they're not connecting with the real, living people who are receiving their ads.

Many marketers discuss their audience like all those people are just robots on the other side of the screen with credit cards, one-dimensional characters that are going to buy things because the marketer did a good job setting up their Facebook ad. But that's just not true. This is why I spend so much time going to live events, doing Facebook Live videos, teaching webinars and interacting with people in private groups. The channel itself doesn't matter, and the tactics themselves don't matter — what matters is connecting and communicating with the people you're serving.

When you spend your time studying things like copy and creative, and understanding how we actually communicate with other people, you'll learn to judge whether your offer is actually going to solve a problem for them. Without an offer that serves them, it doesn't matter how good your ads are.

That's why brands that have decided to serve a specific *market* of people are the most successful over the long-term. Look at a company like Apple — how many different products have they produced over the years? How many times have they adapted and refined their offer to keep up with where their customers are going? They aren't just a technology company. Apple is a company that makes tools for innovators and creators, and that is why they are one of the three most valuable companies in the world. Their focus is about continuing to serve their customers in every area, responding and innovating to keep providing for what their market is interested in — instead of just sticking with something that's easy or that they're already good at. If your business is going to be successful over the long term, you really have to be there to serve your customers and to evolve and adapt as they ask you to.

Now, there are some key principles to marketing that actually *serves* people, and I want to spend the rest of this chapter exploring them, so you have the strongest foundation possible, right from the start.

RESPONSIBILITY IN MARKETING

Not only are we here to serve our customers, but digital marketers also have a huge responsibility to our customers, and to our communities.

Marketing is about understanding the psychology of your customer, and about empathizing with their fears, hopes and self-perceptions, which means that marketers are in an extremely influential position with their audience. Our job is to persuade people to take a particular course of action, and that makes us very powerful. And with that great power comes great responsibility. For example, over 40 million people see Ezra Firestone's ads every year and are affected by his message in some way. Ezra is really aware of the ethical responsibility he has to each of those 40 million people. He knows how big a ripple effect his message can have when so many people are exposed to it, so he's really focused on creating ad messages that are positive and healthy for his audience.

For example, with his cosmetics brand Boom! by Cindy Joseph, the products are well-made, of course, but the thing his audience loves so much is the messaging. The target audience is women over 50, and instead of saying, "Hey, let's get rid of your wrinkles, let's make you look younger" and going with the common anti-aging message, Ezra's team is leading a pro-age revolution. Their message? *"The whole world might be telling you that you're old and that you don't matter, or that you need to deal with your wrinkles, but we think aging is beautiful, we support you and we're helping you embrace the beauty that comes with getting older."*

That's a completely different way to approach that market, and the audience feels so understood and cared for that the company has scaled to over $30 million in revenue each year. Making those customers feel good creates a positive flow-on effect in the world, because those customers feel more confident and happy — instead of the negative flow-on effect that would happen by making them feel insecure or that something about them needs to be fixed.

You might be reading this, especially if you've been in marketing for a while, and thinking to yourself, *"Yeah, but fear sells. Twisting the knife on people's pain points works, because they'll do what it takes to make that pain go away."* And that's true. As humans we are all highly motivated to avoid pain, loss and fear. But the challenge for marketers today is to speak to those pains and fears without manipulating them or making them worse. You can address those problems without making the audience feel broken or attacking them. The messages we marketers put out there can really affect what someone thinks about themselves. This is why many of the major platforms, including Facebook, now have technology to assess whether ads are going to have a positive or negative effect on the audience.

For example, if you upload a Facebook ad, with people smiling outside in the sunshine, the algorithm is going to think it's positive, but if you have a picture of a kid crying, and it's set in a dark room, the algorithm will pick up those negative connotations. That's not to say that negative ads are banned or never get shown, but you are likely to have more success with your ads when they're positive, because Facebook is trying to limit the negative impact the platform has on people.

THE ETHICS OF TAILORED MARKETING

All the platforms we use for digital marketing have tens, sometimes hundreds, of thousands of data points about us. The longer we use the platform and the more active we are online, the more data they amass. For marketers, this is good news. The more information we have, the more specific we can be in who we market to and what we offer them. But this is relatively new territory from an ethical perspective — there has never been another time in history where marketers can impact market behavior so extensively.

Sometimes targeted marketing seems creepy to people who aren't familiar with the technology. For a platform like Facebook, the goal is to aggregate as many eyeballs onto content as possible. It's like a media company or a newspaper or a TV show — they're going to monetize the attention they garner through advertising. But what makes Facebook so powerful is, in part, the depth of their targeting. People share their lives on Facebook. For example, if you went to a Dave Matthews concert, and you purchased his album on iTunes, Facebook knows that you like that band, which in turn becomes data that advertisers can use to run more targeted ads to you.

A lot of people who aren't in marketing don't realize how much data all these platforms have gathered about them. We all agree to the terms of service when we sign up for an account, but many people don't understand that this is the business model — that their free membership allows Facebook to collect these mass amounts of data about them. The price we pay to use the platform is measured in our data instead of our dollars. The data can be restricted to some degree by individual users, but ultimately, the model allows advertisers to use these very targeted interests to reach their audience and that's how Facebook makes money. (And, to be clear, how media buyers make money.)

Generally, I think that the move towards more tailored marketing is a good thing. It's a lot better for consumers to see targeted ads, because those ads are much more relevant than the general marketing that was so common in the past. That generalized approach has caused consumers to become blind to a lot of ads, and to think of advertising and marketing as sleazy, annoying, useless noise.

But when ads are very targeted to their needs, the products or services the customer buys can really enrich their life. If we do good marketing for good products and services, and put those things in front of the people that need it, we can solve a lot of problems for people. When you leverage targeted marketing like that, with a clear sense of ethics, responsibility and care for your audience, it's good for you and it's good for them. Your business will thrive and your customers find the solutions they need and want in order to get more out of life.

WORK ON WHAT MATTERS

Getting ahead in this field is not about just grinding for more hours. While 'hustle' is held up in our culture as the ultimate indicator of success, that mentality leads to a really unhealthy relationship with your work.

Time spent is not an effective measure of how hard you're working. That is an old, outdated framework for measuring productivity, and it goes way back in our history. When the U.S. started to become industrialized, the more hours that people worked in a factory did equal more productivity, because more goods were produced. But if you're a media buyer, or you're working in a digital marketing team, or even a corporate business, you're not clocking hours at a factory. The quality of the time you put in is far more important than the quantity of the hours you put in. There's also a difference between being productive and being effective. Being productive is about ticking things off a list. Being effective is about ticking the right things off the list.

If you're a media buyer, the vast majority of your time should be spent strategizing, building, and optimizing campaigns. If you're a community manager, you should be completely focused on facilitating the success of your customers and audience. If you're a data analyst, your time should be spent immersed in the key metrics of the business, and dreaming about ways to put that data to use.

Do the thing that you're really good at, and ignore the rest. Staying on the computer for an extra hour or two at night to tweak tiny details in a new campaign you've already launched is not productive and it's not effective. Do the work that is necessary and that really matters — the stuff that's going to have a meaningful impact on the business. Leave the rest alone.

LOOKING AFTER YOURSELF (NO LONGER OPTIONAL)

For most people working in teams or on their own businesses, it's pretty obvious that we have a responsibility to our customers and to the people we work with. But so many people forget that we also have a responsibility to ourselves — to our health, our personal relationships, and our own growth and development.

It's easy to lose yourself in this type of work, because you can get totally absorbed in the campaign results and in how the market is behaving. It's very easy to lose sight of the rest of your life, especially because we're working on computers and with technologies that are designed to be very addictive. I've seen so many people get sucked into a never-ending cycle of work online, who lose their connections to the world and their social group, and forget to take care of themselves. Obviously that leads to burnout, and it makes it very hard to continue to use good judgement and empathy when you aren't connected to other people in your personal life.

Taking care of yourself means that you will be able to keep showing up to do awesome work in the digital world. You first have to take care of yourself in the offline world to thrive in the online world.

I think this is so important that we actually created a whole workshop about it called Balanced Being, which you can access for free at mollypittman.com/clickhappy. It covers everything I and other leaders in this space rely on to make sure we have healthy, balanced careers, as well as actionable strategies to help you thrive as a digital professional.

It might seem like a weird thing to cover in a book about digital marketing, but I promise that looking after yourself will pay off in your work — you'll be more focused, more productive and more physically capable of doing everything you need to. There's nothing more important than this. We are meant to have a connection to nature. We are meant to exercise and eat good foods, to have engaging and meaningful experiences with family and friends, and to have time alone, away from all our gadgets.

So, how do we look after ourselves? For me, it's come to three key changes.

1. Take care of your body.

Diet and exercise are also so important, because you function better all round when you're moving your body and fuelling it right. Exercise is also like meditation for me — usually you're away from technology, so that's a great experience to have each day. Taking care of your body obviously makes you feel good, but it also builds your self-respect and self-esteem. If you want others to respect you, particularly in your work life, you must also respect yourself, and taking time to look after yourself and your body is a clear indication of that self-respect. Taking care of your body also tends to make you more mindful, so you're going to be more aware when you feel yourself falling down the rabbit hole of technology and reactiveness.

2. Invest in real-life relationships.

Another key is blocking out time to make sure you have social interactions a few times a week — whether that's to meet new people, reconnect with the people you've known forever, or to invest in the most important people in your life. And when you're with those people, just be with them. It's normal and acceptable now to start texting or scrolling when you're with other people, but that's actually really weird. While technology can be an amazing tool, it can also rob us of our ability to be present with people. Being present in each moment, rather than letting your attention wander off to every new notification, makes a huge difference to your mindset, and to the quality of your relationships.

3. Control your tech (and your FOMO).

It is so important not to wake up and immediately go to your technology. When we wake up and instantly open our phones or computers, what we're really looking for is connection with other people. But a text message or an email is an *approximation* of connection, not the real thing. Often, you don't even get that — you just find out that you already have all kinds of things to catch up on, and your day starts with stress. And when you do that day by day, week by week, month by month, it's really easy to lose perspective. Instead, when you wake up, try to take some time for yourself. Instead of flicking through Facebook or Instagram, spend the time reading or meditating, connecting with your loved ones, eating mindfully, and just letting your body wake up and feel good as you start the day.

Our access to technology — smartphones and social media and the 'always-on' flow of information — is very new for humanity. We are the first people in history to deal with this type of technology, and it's why tech addiction is such an issue right now. Platforms like Facebook, and hardware like your iPhone, are built to keep you engaged as long as possible. But all over the world, we're seeing depression, anxiety, and a lot of social issues emerging from the social isolation we're experiencing as a result of all these platforms.

We need to address this now, and set boundaries now, so that we protect our sense of self-worth and confidence, our ability to focus, and our ability to connect deeply with other people. This is key for marketers to understand, both for their own health, and for how they relate to their audience. A study called 'No More FOMO: Limiting Social Media Decreases Loneliness and Depression' published in the *Journal of Social and Clinical Psychology* in 2018 had this to say:

 Given the breadth of research linking social media use to worse well-being, we undertook an experimental study to investigate the role that social media plays in this relationship. After a week of baseline monitoring, 143 undergraduates at the University of Pennsylvania were randomly assigned to either limit Facebook, Instagram and Snapchat use to 10 minutes, per platform, per day, or to use social media as usual for three weeks. The limited use group showed significant reductions in loneliness and depression over three weeks compared to the control group. Both groups showed significant decreases in anxiety and fear of missing out over baseline, suggesting a benefit of increased self-monitoring. Our findings strongly suggest that limiting social media use to approximately 30 minutes per day may lead to significant improvement in well-being.[1]

It seems like a lot of the work that we do in marketing has to be done inside, on the computer, but there are actually lots of opportunities to step away from the computer. I encourage you to look out for those opportunities and to take advantage of them. For example, if you're writing ad copy, close your computer, get a notebook out, and change your environment. Go to a coffee shop with a friend to work, or go outside and sit in the sun, and enjoy that this job allows you that flexibility.

Now that we understand these rules of the new world of work, let's explore the fundamental element of online marketing: the customer journey, and everything that needs to be in place to ensure your business is creating successful customers.

6

THE CUSTOMER VALUE JOURNEY

The Customer Journey is a concept that Ryan Deiss mapped out at DigitalMarketer, and it's a powerful way to understand the foundational principles of marketing. We're going to take that a step further to show how paid traffic then fits into the customer journey.

The first thing to understand is that marketing is about building a relationship with your customers. And just as there are effective and ineffective ways to build healthy, happy relationships with people in your personal life, there are effective and ineffective ways to build relationships with your customers online.

Many marketers are too much, too soon for their customers. They have a product or service, set up a Facebook ad, run it to cold traffic (people who have never heard of them before) and assume that all those people will buy. But that almost never works, and the reason is that as consumers, we behave very similarly online as we do in person. Even though we're online, we still have to build that relationship with someone before we ask them for a big commitment. It's like going on a first date with someone: if you start suggesting names for your future children before you've even gotten to dessert, it's too much, too soon.

Other marketers are overcompensating for something, and never get out of the 'friend zone': they give so much value first, but never get around to asking for the sale. Some marketers are way too pushy, and others are not pushy enough. Understanding the customer journey will help you avoid falling into either trap.

Here's how Ryan describes the customer journey:

> The customer journey is simply a visual acknowledgement of what's already happening. We're not talking about *causing* something to happen; we're just documenting what's already happening, so that we can make it happen more efficiently. We want to take a customer all the way through from initial awareness to success, so that they do not merely become a customer, and not merely a happy customer, but a customer who has been fundamentally changed for the better as a result of doing business with you.
>
> There are all kinds of models out there to visualize customer journeys. The one we developed has eight stages. It starts with awareness — how do they become aware that your brand exists? Do they see an ad, find you in search results, or hear of you by word of mouth? Awareness alone though is not enough, especially online, so that's why step two is Engage. If someone doesn't get to engage with you, then you just paid for a click that's going to be worth nothing to you.

Engagement happens through content, through social channels, and through follow-up marketing (like an email newsletter). If someone is reading a blog post, watching a video or subscribing to your list, they're beginning to engage with the brand. A lot of businesses skip this stage (and sometimes even Stage One) and try to take people who have never heard of them or engaged with any part of their business straight to Stage Three or Four.

Stage Three is Subscribe, and this is where you've gotten the ability to follow up — like in any relationship, where you get their details so you can be in touch. This is where the prospect gives you permission to follow up with them.

Stage Four is Convert. We're not looking for a massive purchase here, we're just looking for a micro-commitment. This is where the prospect buys something, or they make a significant time commitment. They buy a small product or service, or they sign up for a demo or webinar. Humans show commitment with their wallets and calendars. They're giving you a valuable resource — money or time — which indicates they're ready to do business with you. Before trying to sell anything big, you want to see that your leads, no matter how qualified, are starting to make some micro-commitments.

Stage Five is the Excite stage, which acknowledges that if you had a good first interaction, it's time to ask for a second. It's about asking how we as marketers can ensure that every new customer gets a little victory out of their micro-commitment, so that they're inclined to go one step further. This stage is also very commonly missed, and it's about customer success, ensuring the customer actually gets what they wanted out of that transaction, and that they consume the product, so they internalize the value of it. This stage prevents buyer's remorse, and sets you up for Stage Six.

Assuming someone is excited about the product, they'll move on to Stage Six, Ascension, which can include upsells, cross-sells, and recurring subscriptions. This stage is about getting your new customer to do more. They just purchased something, they're pumped up about it, so what other things can you offer them to ascend them through your company's value journey? This can happen over time — all these offers don't have to be in one funnel — but you want to make sure that you aren't only focused on the first Convert stage and forget about all the other opportunities you have with each customer. Stages Six through Eight are really untapped territory for most businesses, because everyone focuses on the first few stages and forgets about the back end.

Stage Seven is Advocacy, where customers say nice things about you to other people. This usually starts happening as they become successful and have real results to show from having worked with you. They've had a good experience with your business and they're making small efforts to reward you.

Stage Eight is the level of Active Promotion. When someone reaches this stage, they're moving far beyond the level of advocacy. As a promoter they're taking your brand on as a part of their identity. These are the Harley Davidson owners that have a Harley Davidson tattoo. People like this don't just buy the new iPhone, they're the ones camping out to get it. These are your top affiliates and value-added resellers. They're not just leaving you reviews or giving you testimonials — they're more excited about your brand than you are. This is why marketing needs to be responsible not just for producing customers, not just producing happy customers, but producing successful customers.

The value journey consists of multiple marketing campaigns, and they all work together to move someone up the chain from Awareness to Active Promotion. No matter what type of marketing you're using — direct mail, email marketing, paid traffic — you need to ensure that you have content and a campaign in place for each of the eight stages. One campaign hands a prospect or customer directly onto the next one, so it's a smooth transition that never lets anyone fall through the cracks.

Unfortunately, most businesses have one marketing campaign, with four or five goals — awareness, generating leads, getting conversions, making profit — and it's just too much for one campaign to deliver. Other businesses focus exclusively on the front end, and never spends any time building the back end campaigns that would increase the average order value and total lifetime value of each customer.

As a rule of thumb, I believe that every business should have at least one campaign for every three steps in the journey. While it's ideal to have a campaign for each individual stage, if you're just getting started, at least create a campaign that covers the first three stages: Aware, Engage and Subscribe. Then create a campaign that moves someone through Convert, Excite and Ascend, then another that takes them right through Advocacy and Promotion. Each campaign needs content that sends traffic to a specific location, and a traffic source that finds those people and leads them to engage with the content.

Now that you've got a clear idea of what the customer value journey is, and how it provides a framework you can build your different types of marketing campaigns around, you can use it like an assembly line. It's a clear model for mapping out the campaigns, content and traffic strategies that will allow you to continually turn unaware prospects into customers who love and promote your brand.

Now you understand the job of a campaign, but what does that term actually mean? Well, there are five elements involved in any successful paid media campaign: creating an offer, writing your copy, developing creative, building your targeting and creating your 'ad scent' (and we'll get into each of these over the next few chapters). All of these elements work together to create a cohesive, 'sticky' experience for the customer, where they are getting clear messaging from you and have a consistent experience from the moment they first see your ad, through to buying your product or service. All of them are equally important and you have to have each piece in place if you're going to build reliable and replicable campaigns. People want to get caught up in the tactical button-pressing side of media buying and while that's important, if you always go back to the basics and focus on these five things, your campaigns will always be much more likely to succeed.

7

MEET THE MEDIA BUYER

If you Google "digital media buyer," there are terrible explanations of what that role is, so let me clear it up real quick: a media buyer aggregates and purchases attention. Media buyers connect consumers with brands that may be of service or interest to them.

Good media buyers don't think of people as robots we can sell trinkets to. We dig deep into understanding the people we are selling to, so that we can be honest about whether they really want or need what we are selling. Is the product good? Does it deserve to be out in the market? These are really important questions that you need to get comfortable answering to be a good media buyer — if you don't, you can end up with a moral conflict about what you're working on, and that will absolutely affect how you perform.

Again, this role is so much more than pressing buttons on Facebook. Media buyers are powerful. We bring new life to businesses, and we can change the world through our influence. Our messages can be shown to millions of real people, and as I said earlier, that's a huge responsibility. In this role, you are personally going to create the messages people will absorb and the actions they will take, and I never want you to forget the privilege and responsibility this is. Use these powers for good, not evil!

Media buyers perform one of the most important functions within a business. Bringing in new leads and customers is incredibly valuable, and once you develop that skill set, you can apply it to any kind of business, and no one can take it away from you. The ability to bring new customers in the door is one of the most powerful levers a business can pull on to grow, and as you master this skill, you become invaluable.

Traditional marketing, like print ads, billboards and even physical in-store marketing can be hard to measure and track, and there's really no opportunity for the customer to get the level of interaction they want. In digital marketing we have very specific statistics and metrics we can track — how many people visited a certain page, how many people converted, and so on — and so it's making marketing a much more technical skill than it ever has been before.

This role is about far more than just buying the actual media. When I look at all the people who are successful in this field, there are some common features.

- First of all, we are marketers: we understand data, funnel architecture and the levers to pull in any business to create growth.
- We are psychologists: we understand what our market feels, needs, wants and fears.
- We are researchers: we are willing to do a lot of research to find the answers we need about our audiences and campaigns.
- We are empaths: we understand that we are just

humans connecting with other humans — we're not day traders buying stocks, we're immersing ourselves in shared human experience to develop a deep sense of connection and respect with our audience.

- We are communicators: we translate between a brand, the offers they have, and the market they can help.

Our job as media buyers is to purchase and aggregate the attention of those markets, from the sources that are most relevant. Paid traffic is like the road that connects all the people online (coming from sources like Facebook, Google and YouTube) with the product or service being offered by the brand you are working with. Our job is to send traffic along this road. We get to decide which road we want to send the traffic down, what kind of traffic we want to send, and how we want that traffic to travel.

HOW TO THINK LIKE A MEDIA BUYER

Each role in a digital marketing team — the email marketer, copywriter, data analyst, content marketer — is uniquely valuable, but most of the time, the media buyer is the only person on the team who is actually spending money to acquire customers. This creates a unique set of challenges, so whether it's your money (because you own the business) or it's your employer's money, you have to build the mindset that allows you to protect and maximize that money. There are eight steps to learn in order to think like a world-class media buyer, who protects the investment in paid traffic.

As you progress through this book, and go out and start your campaigns, come back to these steps whenever you need to put your media buyer hat on. Come back to this part if you're stuck on an ad or you're feeling overwhelmed with how complex everything seems.

1: MIND CLEAN-UP

I've met so many media buyers who are very data-focused button-clickers. They are really good at scaling and optimization and duplicating their ads, but they hit a ceiling with their success. This is because they're carrying around a whole lot of 'head trash.' Media buying is totally a mental game, which is why I meditate each day before I start working to clear out all this junk.

FEAR OF FAILURE

If you're just starting out, or you've had a tough stretch with your ads, having some failed ads can really hurt your confidence. The fear of failure can stop you from being creative and from launching new things.

To address this, the solution might be as simple as giving yourself a pep talk, meditating, looking back at some earlier wins, or talking to someone you respect — but whatever you do, you have to deal with it. Try to keep in mind that there's never *really* a failed marketing campaign: the only reason a marketing campaign fails is when it's really half-assed. If you don't put proper time and effort into it, then it's no surprise if the campaign fails, but if you've put in the work and the campaign doesn't achieve what you want, you're still getting data and you're still learning. If the campaign teaches you something about the offer and the audience, it's not a true failure.

MONEY ISSUES

When I was starting out, I really had a lot of weird beliefs about money. My job is to spend other people's money, and that can be scary. A scarcity-driven mindset around money holds a lot of media buyers back, and I have seen many marketers who have bad-ass campaigns but never scale, because they're afraid to spend more money. They're worried that if they lose any money, they'll never get it back. But in this business, you're going to lose money, and you're going to make it too — often more than enough to cover the losses. This is normal in paid media. Once you address any of those fears or beliefs then the floodgates can open. I recommend people like Gabby Bernstein and Chris Harder as resources for developing a healthier money mindset.

Need for Validation

In this role, you need to decide what success looks like to you. This has nothing to do with the KPIs of the role — it's about what you need, in order to feel good about your work. You need to know what it means to you personally, because if you are looking for validation from someone else, you will be unfulfilled.

Everyone's expectations are different. Are you launching campaigns with an expectation of validation or approval from someone else, or are you doing it for yourself, with the mindset of meeting your own expectations? If you can make that shift, it frees you to make decisions simply because you want to be the best media buyer you can be, not because you're trying to impress someone.

2: DETERMINE THE MESSAGE YOU'RE SHARING

Most people go straight to focusing on the specific

product or service they're going to put in their ad. I want you to focus on the fact that you're buying attention. The message of a brand, or the story behind the person who started the brand, is often so much more powerful than a single product.

For example, my friend Roxelle runs Fused Hawaii Bikinis — she makes really cool swimsuits from recyclable goods that are designed to fit surfers and other outdoorsy people. Her message is so much more than the product is on its own — that you don't need the 'perfect body,' that you should be free to live confidently in the skin you're in. Well, she can't spend enough on Facebook ads or keep up with the incredible demand for her products!

Roxelle didn't just ask what product she was going to take to the market, she asked what message she wanted to send people, and she wanted to present herself as the ambassador for that message. Her product is simply an extension of that personal brand and message, which is why it's been so successful.

3: GET INTO THE MINDSET OF THE MARKET

Whenever I start working with a new market, I will give myself at least a few hours to just search around the Internet, looking for where the market hangs out and what they pay attention to. I join Facebook groups, read blogs, look at forums, read Amazon reviews of relevant products, watch webinars. If I can go to a live event or talk to live people, I will absolutely do that too. I know that I've done a good job of this when nearly every ad I see in my Facebook feed for the next few weeks is related to that market.

Again, we're not diving into tactical stuff like targeting yet. At this stage, we're just trying to get a sense of who these people are, what they think about, what they stress about, what they are happy about, what their desires are, what words they use, and what type of stuff they buy.

4: IDENTIFY WHY THEY WILL CARE

Why does this market want to hear this message? This might take you five minutes or it might take you hours to capture, but let's go back to Roxelle and her bathing suits. She can immediately go to this market of women — moms, surfers, explorers who want to feel good in their bodies — and ask why they would want to hear the message she is going to share.

Maybe they want to set a good example for their kids, or they're sick of logging into Facebook every day and seeing ads of unrealistic body types. Or even if they're happy with their body, maybe they're struggling with self-confidence because none of the bathing suits they find are designed to suit their shape. You've got to take the time to list these reasons, because not only does it make you more empathetic to your market, but these reasons will provide the hooks for a lot of your ads later on.

5: DECIDE HOW THE OFFER WILL BE PRESENTED

If you haven't read *Big Magic* by Elizabeth Gilbert, I highly recommend it. That book really changed me as a media buyer, in terms of actually learning how to be creative. 'Be creative' is such an intangible instruction, especially if you don't think of yourself as creative, but it's so important in this role. A large part of creativity in media buying is allowing yourself the time that's necessary — time away from the computer to let ideas come to you as you ask yourself how this message should be presented to the market in a way that will resonate. What are the visual ways to present the message? What are the words and ideas to use? This is where you start thinking about the copy and creative, how you visually represent what your brand is about.

6: LAUNCH YOUR CAMPAIGNS

After you've gone through the first five steps, it's time to do something with all the data and ideas and get a campaign out there. Elizabeth Gilbert talks about this in *Big Magic* too — writer's block (which in this case we can call media buyer's block) often happens because you've generated so many ideas and not put any of them into action. When I was working at DigitalMarketer, one of our 'We Believe' statements was that "half-ass is better than no ass" — even if something isn't perfect, get it out the door. And while I don't want you to half-ass your campaigns, I don't want you to do nothing at all, either. So at this stage, get something out there. Keep yourself moving so the block of too many ideas and not enough action doesn't catch up with you.

7: ANALYZE THE RESULTS

This is our biggest learning step, and it's often the scariest step for people, because it seems like the moment they'll discover if they did a good job or a bad job. Erase that from your mind. Forget about good or bad. Of course we have goals that we want to hit, but every campaign is a gift, because you get so much data to tell you what to do differently next time. So many people skip this step because they don't want to look at the hard facts, in case they don't like what they see. But you will learn far more from analyzing what you've done than you will from reading this book, taking any training or listening to any podcast, because you will be practically applying your knowledge, rather than just learning more theory.

8: ITERATE, COLLABORATE, AND KEEP MOVING FORWARD

As media buyers, we are always iterating. At DigitalMarketer, I calculated that only about 20% of the campaigns that I launched succeeded at hitting the CPA (cost per acquisition) goal. That's still good to me, because we learned something from the remaining 80% of campaigns — and because you don't need every campaign to be a success. Our real goal in this role is to get the message out there, and then to keep iterating and improving. If something doesn't work, don't give up. Often collaboration is the best resource for fixing something you're stuck on, so if you try something and it doesn't work, talk to people. Post in Facebook groups, get on a call with a mentor or another media buyer, talk to your team, find a way to collaborate. By Step Eight, you can end up being so close to the data that you can't see what's right in front of you. Other people can point those things out to you, and even if the problem isn't obvious, they will often have ideas that can help you keep moving forward.

8

WINNING OFFERS & STELLAR
AD COPY

In order for a business to function, it has to offer a product or service. When we're talking about an offer here, we're not talking about the actual thing your business sells — your *product* might be a cool piece of software, but your *offer* might be the free 14-day trial that encourages prospects to buy the product.

Your role as a media buyer is to help develop an offer that puts your product or service into the hands of your customers. And as simple as it sounds, the number one factor in any successful paid ad campaign is to make sure that the offer you make is something your audience will actually want.

The offer is the vehicle that takes them from the 'before state' to the 'after state.'

Imagine you're staring at your living room. It's drab — no art and no interesting furniture. You feel flat and boring, like no one would want to hang out there with you.

Now imagine replacing your couch with something vintage and funky.

Then — and this is the most important part — imagine

people in the living room, laughing and hanging out on that couch with you!

This is the transformation from 'before' to 'after' — the 'after' state isn't about the product itself. It's about experiencing the shift from feeling lonely and down to feeling happy and cared for.

So when you're thinking about your offer and your copy, ask yourself: What is it about your offer that provides a transformation for the end user? How are you taking them from a dissatisfied 'before state' to a happy and satisfied 'after state'? The kind of offer you make is certainly going to be business-specific, but a lot of the success of an offer depends on making this psychological transformation clear to the audience.

That's where copy comes in. Your copy (the words and language you use in your ads and content) is where you articulate *why* the offer is something the market wants. The offer and copy go hand-in-hand. Once you know which product you are going to make an offer for, and what that transformative hook will be, the copy should just about write itself.

The first rule of writing good ad copy is that it's not about you — it's about your prospects and customers. We're all so caught up in our own ideas and goals for our businesses that a lot of the ad copy we write can end up being very self-promotional. We end up fixating on why our product or service is so great, instead of focusing on what it will do for our audience. And while we obviously want our prospects to know how good the product is, that product-focused approach absolutely does not work on social platforms.

It's got to be prospect-focused, so whenever I sit down to write copy, I always like to imagine that one of those real-life people from my audience is sitting right across the table from me, waiting for me to connect with them. I try to think about how they would respond to everything I'm writing down and whether this copy would get their interest and make them want to know more. When you can come from a place of empathy and real connection to your audience, your ad copy will be so much better than if you sit down with the mindset that it's time to sell as hard as you can.

Hard-sell ad copy doesn't usually generate a lot of social proof (likes, comments or shares) and so these ads are not ranked well in the auctioning system Facebook uses to display ads to its users. If you write very hypey sales copy, your costs are going to be high, your reach will be low, and you won't get the results you want.

Two-thirds of Facebook's algorithm is oriented towards the user experience, so you really have to try to get into the heart and mind of your customers so that you can position your offers to really resonate with them. We are all wired to filter information according to how it will benefit us individually, so if your copy and your offer don't seem specifically relevant, people will ignore it.

That's why your copy should be as personable and actionable as possible, particularly on Facebook and the other social platforms. People are used to scrolling through their newsfeeds to see content from their family, friends and colleagues — they're not there to look at ads from brands (unless they're marketing nerds like me!). If you can accommodate the mental state they're in at the moment they see your ad, your audience will be much more likely to respond positively. Making your copy very personal, as if you were talking to a friend, works very well for most businesses online.

The more personal you can be, the more people are going to respond to your ad, the more they're going to share it, and the higher your relevance score will become (which in turn means that your ad will be shown to greater numbers of people).

A huge mistake that people make on ad platforms is that they try to be too professional. A more relaxed, fun, human touch is what really works on social platforms — like the ad is a post from a friend.

The length and style of your copy are both variables to test with your particular offer and audience. I've seen very short, witty ads do very well, and I've seen heartfelt multi-paragraph ads work well too (though if you do go for longer copy, make sure your call to action isn't buried at under seven paragraphs of text — put it earlier, because most people won't make it that far). It really depends on where you're at in the customer journey with this audience segment. Really, the answer to how long your ad should be is as long as it takes to get your point across.

Don't overthink this. If you can write a text message to a friend or chat with someone comfortably in Messenger, you're going to be able to write some pretty good Facebook ad copy, even if you don't think you're a great writer normally. Just keep it simple, make your point, and test different variations when you start getting some traction.

MARKETING HOOKS

A marketing hook is the compelling reason that encourages a prospect or customer to take you up on the offer you're making. It's far deeper than the features or benefits of the offer; it's the thing that makes them realize exactly why that offer is relevant to them personally.

Your ad copy, then, is the articulation of that hook. This is also done through your creative (the images and design you use, which we'll talk more about later), but your copy should explain why your offer is something the market wants. We want to…

- Quickly convey why this offer matters to the market.
- Be relevant to the target audience: the reason someone wants to consume your offer will vary depending on who they are, so different ads need different copy to speak to each of those specific motivations.
- Look like an organic post. Most folks will change the TV channel, skip the pre-roll on YouTube, and hide the ad in their newsfeeds when they see obvious ads. The less your ad *looks* like an ad, the better. Focusing on writing ads that actually create engagement will create a better user experience, and will indicate to Facebook that this campaign deserves a high-value placement in the display auction.

A great sales message simply articulates the shift the customer goes through from the 'before' state to the 'after' state. Keep this in mind when you sit down to think about the marketing hooks you can build your ad copy around. The 'before' state and 'after' state will vary greatly between businesses, but there's always a transformation involved in every offer.

What does the prospect have in the 'before' state that they would like to trade for something different in the 'after' state? How do they feel in the 'before' state? What is their average day like as a result of being stuck in the 'before' state? What is the 'before' state doing to their social status? Which of their value sets is being compromised by staying in the 'before' state?

Then think about the answers to those same questions once they've shifted to the 'after' state: what do they have now? How do they feel? What is their average day like as a result of this shift, and what's their status now? How have those values been transformed?

I usually try to test three different versions of ad copy to each audience segment to see what resonates most, and iterate over time as I get to know what makes those segments respond best.

CHUNKY COPY

I'm going to share some ideas you can use to start generating copy for your own business, but first I want to make a note that the very first priority in writing ad copy for social platforms is to generate social proof.

When you write your copy, make sure it's something people want to engage with, to comment on and share, because the more social proof the ad gets, the higher it will be ranked by Facebook's ad algorithm, which optimizes for which ads are generating the most traffic. (I cover this in detail in Train My Traffic Person with Ezra Firestone. You can get details and other amazing resources at mollypittman.com/clickhappy)

This engagement is why native ads (an ad that just looks like normal content for the platform) tend to perform best across all the social platforms. When you take off your 'professional copywriter hat' and just write as if you're posting on your personal profile or speaking to a friend, you'll see a lot more success with your ads.

There are many different hooks you can use to write social ad copy. In this section I'm going to briefly explain the five different hooks I rely on most often for writing ad copy for my clients and my own products.

We open the body text with the hook — whichever part of the 'before' state or 'after' state you're focusing on. This should always be right at the start of the ad, since it's what will get your prospect's attention most effectively.

Next, you want to position your offer or call to action as the vehicle that will move the prospect through that transformation from the 'before' state to the 'after' state. The headline mirrors the hook, or simply states what they will get from your offer, and every hook ends in a call to action.

Let's dive into each of the big angles I like best when developing ad copy for social campaigns. I call these copy chunks.

---

1. PAIN/BENEFIT CHUNK

This model speaks to the 'before' state, right at the beginning of the copy. You speak directly to the thing that's getting your prospect down. "Ever wish...?" "Tired of...?" "Are you struggling to...?" Then in the second part of the copy, you show them the transformation that's possible with your offer. "Do this... and get that" or "Get this... and achieve that."

Of course, you need to flesh this out a bit so that the copy is more conversational, but this is a simple structure you can use to get started. This is a very traditional approach, and I use it a lot, because it's simple and it works. You can use any of the 'before' and 'after' states that we talked about earlier with this structure.

For example: *"Tired of your dog going crazy every time it sees something new? Take our quiz about dog behavior and find out how to help your dog calm down for good in just three steps."*

. . .

2. 'HAVE' CHUNK

This is about addressing what the prospect has in their 'before' state and what they will have in the 'after' state if they take the action you are offering. "Having [bad thing] is [a bad feeling]... that's why we made [your offer here]. Get [offer] and experience [good feeling or transformation]." This is similar to the Pain/Benefit chunk, but we change the focus to something they have that's undesirable, that they can trade for something they really want.

For example: *"Having dead grass and weeds in your yard isn't a good look. Want a gorgeous green lawn instead? Watch this video to find out how we can help you get the best garden on your block."*

3. 'FEEL' CHUNK

Personally, I love this option because I'm an empath and it helps me to imagine exactly how someone is feeling to write good copy for them. By speaking to someone's feelings, you can connect with them really quickly. In just about every market, with every product or service, there's some element that's connected to how your prospect is feeling.

Whether the change you're providing seems deeply meaningful or not, there are still going to be feelings involved in some way. "Are you feeling ['before' state feeling] because of [pain point]? That's why we made [your offer]. Get this and get ['after' state feeling].

For example: *"Do you feel anxious and overwhelmed every time you have to go to the grocery store? Watch this video to see if you're in our delivery zone and enjoy the peace of mind of having professionals take all the stress out of feeding your family."*

4. AVERAGE DAY CHUNK

The average day hook is about how you are making their

life easier. If you can show someone that you're going to save them time, make something easier or simply that something in their day-to-day life will improve if they take this particular action, that can be really powerful. Things like "Tired of [annoying thing from 'before' average day]? Do/get [your offer] and get [great transformation to 'after' average day]."

For example: *"Are you tired of spending hours in traffic driving to work, day in and day out? Click here to get a month free on your neighbourhood's new bus route, and get an hour back every day to spend on the things you really care about."*

5. STATUS CHUNK

All humans are driven, to some extent, by their ego and by their status in their social group. "Want to be [desirable attribute]? Take this [offer] and start to [benefit]." This one won't work for every business, but it can be powerful if you have an offer where you can position yourself above a mainstream competitor, or where you can show someone how your offer will raise their status in a meaningful way.

For example: *"Want to become an indispensable part of your company's marketing team? Become a certified media buyer with Train My Traffic Person, and develop the skills that will make you absolutely invaluable to any team."*

Use these copy chunks whenever you need inspiration for a marketing campaign. Remember that different angles will resonate with different people in your market, so it's always great to test more than one option.

9

HIGH PERFORMING CREATIVE

Ad creative is the visual aspect of your ad — how it actually looks. Many marketers really overlook their creative, and I think that's often because they don't know what to do about it. I get it — I'm not artistic at all, and can barely tell which colors go together, but I do understand the hooks and emotions we're trying to create. If I can explain that to a designer, we can collaborate to develop the kind of impactful creative I need to make my ads thrive.

Your creative says as much about your chosen hook as your copy, your targeting, or any other part of your system. Your creative is not just the video or image you're using — it's the visual representation of your ad copy. You've heard over and over again that a picture says a thousand words, and it's true: people instantly understand something when they see it, so you should spend at least as much time and effort developing your creative as you spend on writing the copy or doing your targeting research.

Creative includes the layout of the text, the video, the images — whatever visual elements you are using for your ads. We have GIFs now, and carousels of images; there are lots of different ways you can present your ads, and this is where many marketers get lazy. People create really bad-ass campaigns and then just slap a boring stock photo on it at the final moment — it is such a waste!

This is the element of the ad that is most going to catch people's attention, and it's not just about making them glance at the ad for a second — it's about capturing their attention because this offer relates to them so powerfully.

You can never be sure which ad type will resonate with each part of your market — carousel, video, or image. Some consumers are more likely to engage with video, while others, like me, prefer image-based creative. It's best to launch as many campaigns as possible utilizing all three options, as this will guarantee you the greatest reach.

I really recommend putting a lot of research and thought into your creative before you launch your campaign, because this is one of your biggest opportunities. So many people are visual learners, which means that a large part of your audience segment is going to rely on the creative to understand your offer. Your creative can say as much as your copy does, so when you're writing your copy, you also need to come up with a message that can be communicated through visuals.

Many of my students in Train My Traffic Person and at live events have questions about which type of creative is best for ad campaigns, and the answer is that no one type is better than all the others. All of them work — carousel images, single images, videos, slideshows and collections all have their place. The answer to which type of creative is best always depends on your market, your ad, your offer and your hook.

For example, if I'm going to tell a story in my ad, I usually choose a carousel so that I can show multiple images that show change over time. Single-image ads and single-video ads are the most widely used, and I would argue that you need to test both in your ad sets, but it always depends on your audience and offer. The medium is there to support the message, so think about what you're trying to achieve with your ad and choose the format that's going to best support that goal.

Here's what not to do: Don't upload a stock image of a cute animal that has nothing to do with your offer or audience. I still see people do this all the time, and it just doesn't work. It might have worked five or ten years ago, when hypey, over-the-top creative was used just to get people's attention, but consumers (and Facebook) require so much more from us now. Using a picture of a cat doing something funny might get people to briefly stop scrolling, but it's not going to be a qualified click and you're unlikely to get them to convert on your offer.

And don't just show an image of your product or offer. You need to incorporate your marketing message into the image in a way that shows why this offer is relevant to your audience. The image should position the product in the end user's mind so effectively that they don't even have to read the ad copy — they immediately get what it is, get the benefit and can see that it's made especially for them.

CREATIVE GOALS

In the last chapter, we talked about the power of showing people the transformation from the 'before' state to the 'after' state. With your ad creative, you have another opportunity to do this visually, which reinforces (and sometimes outperforms) what you're saying in the copy.

There are a few things your visual creative should do in every campaign.

First, it should tell your audience something — it should convey the marketing hook immediately. This is so much more important than color and design, or even how pretty the ad looks. While a very polished design can help improve the trust the end user has for the brand, clearly communicating the hook is by far the most important thing.

Next, it should be visually appealing enough that the user wants to stop scrolling through their newsfeed. You don't want it to look like an ad — as we talked about in the last chapter, we want it to be native. That means no stock images, no flashing lights, no big arrows. As consumers, the type of media we're used to engaging with comes from our family and friends, so it's the easiest type of ad to engage with too. And because the images and videos that work look like they were taken on an iPhone, you don't have to rely so much on designers anymore (though there will always be cases for working with a designer, particularly if you're looking for a nice text overlay, an illustration or a video.)

Your creative should also be on brand. Even if you're very early in the process of building your business, at this stage you need to start thinking about what your brand looks like from the outside. Most people are going to need to see our ads several times before they decide to take action (this is known as 'effective frequency', and the actual number of exposures required varies between industries). If you have a certain color scheme or design style you use, make sure there's congruence between the existing branding and your ad campaigns (even when you're focusing on very native-style ad creative). You want someone who is engaging with you for the first time to be able to recognize your brand, even if they've only seen you promoting different offers.

Finally, when possible, it should play off associations with visual messages that already exist in our culture. When someone is scrolling through their feed, we have one to three seconds to catch their attention and get them to engage with our ad. So if we can play off any existing icons, symbols, memes — any visual representation where the customer has already assigned context and understanding in their mind — it allows us to get a message across much faster.

One year at DigitalMarketer we were selling tickets for the Traffic & Conversion Summit, and we wanted to communicate the scarcity being created by the tickets starting to run out. I had an idea that everyone viewing the ad would be on an electronic device, so everyone would have the shared context of the battery symbol, and that as the battery goes down, something bad happens — your phone dies, or we run out of tickets! The first ad showed a battery drained to fifty percent, with the remaining amount and the call to action in the regular battery green. The last ad showed the battery drained right down to the last few percent, with the remaining amount and the call to action in that warning red we all know. This worked so well — it was the most successful ad set we ever ran to sell event tickets. The sole reason was that we were able to instantly portray the scarcity hook through the ad creative.

Some of the most effective pieces of creative are simple before-and-after comparison images. You can have the images side by side, or you can make the two images into a GIF that flips back and forth for a few seconds to show the transformation. You can instantly see what the product does — even if the product is not shown in the creative. Think about how you can display the 'before' state, and the 'after' state, and then switch between the two.

Whenever I'm thinking about creative, I always take big keywords from the ad copy or themes that I want to portray and type them into Google. Then I click the image tab to see what images are ranking at the top of the page, which shows me what people are clicking most often when searching for those words.

(Google knows better than anyone what the visual representation of those words is going to be, because they're indexing the Internet — they know how many people have clicked on this certain image in relation to that search term.)

This is a great research process to start building ideas for the visual representation of the transformation you're trying to articulate through your visuals.

When it comes to the actual development of the ad creative, you have a few options. A few years ago I would've said you have to work with a designer because it needs to look high-end, but that's not the case anymore. You just need to be able to relate to your audience. That means you can either create them on your own, or have custom images made (though remember that they often look more like an ad instead of looking native).

If you're having custom images made, then it's wise to work with a designer. Just keep in mind that your designer is not a marketer. Your designer is trained to create beautiful works of art, so it's not enough to send them a landing page and say, "Hey, create ads for this." You need to give them direction, and that's why it's so important that you, as the marketer, set the strategy first. Do you want the pieces of creative to be personal photos or do you want cartoons? What do you want them to portray? How do you want them to look from a style perspective? These directions will help the designer understand what you're looking for from a marketing standpoint. This helps you get better creative, faster, as well as protecting your relationship with your designer by keeping communication clear.

10

LASER TARGETING & AD SCENT

In this chapter, we're going to do a deep dive on targeting, but before we get into it, I want to give you a brief overview of what targeting is in case you're unfamiliar with the idea, followed by an introduction to ad scent, because the two must work together if your campaigns are going to be successful.

Targeting is so important and a lot of marketers struggle here, especially on Facebook. It's so important because you can build an awesome ad campaign with wonderful copy and creative and offer, but if you put it in front of the wrong people it's not going to work, because it wasn't built for them.

The really common mistake here is that people set their targeting to be too broad. When you go to Facebook to set up an ad campaign, you target your ads based on interests, which are data points that Facebook has collected based on what people have shown interest in through their profile. So if the company running ads is selling yoga clothing, for example, most people would just go into the ad manager, type 'yoga' into the interest search bar and target the 30 million or so people in the world who have shown interest in yoga on Facebook.

But that's not the best place to start, because that's not the core, avid part of the market. There's a big difference between someone who's done yoga a couple of times in their life and someone who does yoga every day. Which one of those people do you think is more likely to buy yoga products? It's probably the one that does yoga every day. We want to reach the core part of the market, not just anyone that's ever shown interest.

That's why you must do research. Just start typing keywords into the search box to see what's available, and eventually you will be able to niche down further and further until you find the core of the market. In this example, maybe that's targeting people who like a specific style of yoga, or have shown interest in teacher training. Even if you *are* the avatar you are targeting, you still want to use this research process so that you can find as many interests as possible inside of Facebook to target, to reach this core part of your market.

It's really important to first do a ton of research on the avatar you want to reach. What brands or authority figures does this market look up to? Where do they get their information? If you target based on those types of interest, you're going to come much closer to your core than just targeting a single point of interest.

When it's time to take all that research and set up my ad sets, I start at the top of the interest list I've created. I start building the first ad set and include as many interests as I need to get to a potential audience size of 500,000 to 3 million people. Depending on the size of the interests, this may mean that the ad set has two interests or twenty — it doesn't matter to me, because it's all about obtaining the optimal potential audience size that Facebook prioritizes. As soon as I hit that number, I move on to building the second ad set and continue down my list of interests.

If you'd like to see a list of targeting options I came up with for a past client, you can grab my targeting sheet at mollypittman.com/clickhappy.

THE THREE-PART TRAFFIC SCALE

There are three groups of people you will want to show ads to at various stages of your campaigns. There's cold traffic (people who have never heard of you before), and this is the most important aspect of targeting — making sure your cold traffic is really dialled in.

Retargeting of warm traffic (people who have already engaged with you or been in your ecosystem) and hot traffic (people who have bought from you) is much easier, because you already know who they are and can just set up custom audiences to target them.

Targeting is really about being in tune with your avatar, understanding who wants to buy your products, and why. That's a big question, but being able to answer this question is what makes someone a great marketer. This might come through experience — you've been selling your product and service a long time, and at this stage you just know what kind of person comes to you and what their problems are. Sometimes it's intuition or personal connection to a market, understanding what they're going through on a personal level for some reason.

But a lot of it comes down to research, and that's what we're going to cover in this chapter.

Things have changed a lot in marketing, especially since the Internet has taken off. Today we have a level of opportunity as marketers that has never existed before, but unfortunately, many marketers don't take advantage of what's available to them. Partly that's because you have to go and proactively look for the information — a lot of the opportunity is hidden, and a lot of people just aren't willing to research the volume of data that would make it easy to understand everything about their avatar and market they're serving.

Facebook and Google have *so* much data. Everything can be tracked online, and people are spending so much time on both those platforms, and the platforms are tracking just about every move each user makes. We have never had so much opportunity because people have never been tracked in the way they are now. That's not intended to sound creepy — people have also never expressed themselves so extensively on public platforms where that can be documented. If you loved a band 50 years ago, you would talk to your friends and family about it, and maybe put a poster up in your room. But you weren't posting about that on anything like the Internet, which meant there was no way to market directly to the specific interest you've shown in that music.

And because we have so much data now, we don't have to describe our avatars and markets by their demographics any longer. Normally, when you ask a business owner who they serve, they say things like, "white female, over the age of 50, makes $150k a year and has two kids." They're describing that person on demographic information — what you can see about someone without actually engaging with them — but this is really basic information. It really tells me nothing about that person and what they think about every day.

Years ago, when we just had print ads and billboards, we had to describe our avatars and markets by demographic, because that's all the information we could get. This is not to say that your avatar doesn't *also* fit those demographic points, but these days you need to dig much deeper to get to understand them personally, because that's how you're going to be successful with online ad platforms — they have so much more to provide and a lot of that data also points to purchase intent.

This is something I describe as demographics versus intent. Demographic — age, gender, income — are fine to keep in mind, but it's not something I really ever use in targeting. Of course, there are always exceptions (like if you sell retirement products, for example, you would only want to target people over a certain age), but for most businesses, good targeting comes down to the avatar's intent. Not what they look like, not how much money they make, but what they are interested in, and what their intent is — in life, day-to-day, hour-by-hour.

I like to hear people describe their avatars with comments like, "this person does yoga five times per week", or "they read *Rich Dad, Poor Dad,*" or "they attend the SXSW event in Austin every year" or "they're interested in canning vegetables to save food for their family." Obviously these are just a tiny handful of examples, but all of these are descriptive points about who the avatar is and what motivates them, and it's going to allow you to reach them on Facebook in a much easier way (and keep in mind that I'm using Facebook as the primary example throughout this book, but all these principles hold true across all digital platforms).

So our goal with targeting is to figure out your avatar's intent and then get in front of them on Facebook or wherever we're advertising with a specific offer. We want to be very, very specific, and drill down so far that you know that *only* your market would want to buy this product. I call this the "But No One Else Would' approach to interest targeting. When you're asking yourself questions about your marketing, you need to be able to fill in this statement:

"A _____ enthusiast would know who/what _____ is, but no one else would."

For example, a **golf** enthusiast would know who **Bubba Watson** is, but no one else would. At the time I came up with this idea, Bubba Watson was a successful (but not well-known) golfer. If we were targeting avid golfers, this was a great example of drilling down into that specificity.

Most people in the golf market would target fans of Tiger Woods, reasoning that since he's the biggest golfer ever, there will be a ton of golfers who follow him. Although that might be true, there are also a lot of people who don't play golf, who just follow Tiger because he's famous, or because he's been in the news. My grandmother in Kentucky follows Tiger, just because he's a public figure, and she is most certainly not a golfer! Tiger Woods is not the best interest to target if you're trying to reach golfers, because there are just too many people outside the market who have shown interest.

The next targeting layer down might be Phil Mickelson. He's not as famous as Tiger, but still well-known, so casual *and* avid golfers might have shown interest in him, but you're probably going to knock out most of the people who are just following someone famous. But what you really want is to get down to the layer of people who know who Bubba Watson is. At the time this approach was developed, you would have to follow golf really closely to know that name.

So before you start any campaign, think about which stores your market would shop at that no else would, or what books they would read that no one else would, or who they pay attention to that no one else would.

FACEBOOK'S TARGETING LANDSCAPE

I want to spend a moment here talking about how Facebook sets up its targeting and campaigns. Facebook structures their campaigns so that targeting is determined at the ad set level. When you go into your ads manager, the area listed under Audience is where all this magic happens. The custom audience box is where all of your retargeting audiences are going to live.

This is where your warm and hot traffic will come from, to be used for re-engagement and monetization campaigns. Targeting these two groups is easy-peasy: you can upload customer files (Excel or CSV files of your email list, customer list and so on), and this is also where you can set up retargeting for people who visit your website. You can also create a custom audience of people who use your app, if you have one, and there's even a category called offline activity, where you can upload a list of people who have bought offline, and Facebook will try to match that with your Facebook campaigns to see if any of those purchases were related to your campaigns.

In the Connections field you can also target based on engagement — anyone who likes your page, follows you, likes or comments on posts, engages with your Instagram account or watches your videos.

You can also create look-alike audiences in the custom audiences area. These are audiences you can create for cold traffic, but with a look-alike audience, you're telling Facebook that you want an audience of people that are most like a data point you already have about your market. For example, you could create a look-alike audience of your email list, or of everyone who likes your Facebook page. While these used to be very useful, Facebook changed the data they allocate to look-alike audiences recently and they're no longer strong campaign options. So unless you're already having success with them, it's important that you learn not to rely on these and focus on interest targeting instead.

When it comes to cold traffic, you can target people by where they live, or based on locations where they are spending time or travelling. You can also target everyone in a specific location. That is usually my preference, since you never know what someone is doing in a particular place. Imagine if you were selling tickets to a theatre production in New York City — targeting everyone in NYC would ensure that you show the ad to locals, tourists, and people who have been there recently (and have therefore indicated a willingness to go there). Of course, you would need to add additional targeting to reach interested parties, but it's a good idea to cast a wide net with location. For some businesses, it will make sense to use the other location targets — for example, businesses in the travel space would probably love using the 'people travelling in this location' filter — but for most people, 'everyone in this location' is the best bet.

With the age filters, unless there's a real reason your product or service would only be sold to a certain age range, I almost always just select for 22 years old and above. This is usually the age from which people have discretionary income. It's the same with gender — most campaigns should target both, unless your product or service is very specifically for one or the other, and I never put anything into the languages filter, because so many people speak multiple languages.

The section beneath these very general filters is called Detailed Targeting. When you hit Browse here, you'll see three categories — Demographics, Interests and Behaviors. I really never use anything listed in any of these categories, except for special occasions like anniversaries. Even in the actual Interests category, all the standard options are pretty lame, but you can also just start typing in a word — there are literally hundreds of thousands of interests that Facebook has indexed from all the user activity across the platform. To stick with the yoga example, the easy option would be to click into the Interest category, and just check the 'Yoga' box, but I highly recommend typing in much more specific search terms and relying on the process I'm about to teach you.

I recommend you follow this process even if you've been selling your product for 20 years, because you'll often discover things you never knew existed. Obviously, Google is a big research tool, but you can also use Audience Insights (a research tool from Facebook), and you can read Amazon reviews of other products in the market. If I were trying to get really in tune with that yoga audience, I might go read reviews of yoga mats online, so that I get a sense of what those people care about, what kind of language they use, who they get information from and whose opinions they value. It's the same thing with reading forums and community discussions — join Facebook groups, look for online forums to see what people are talking about, what they're struggling with, what they're thinking about.

THE TARGETING RESEARCH PROCESS

In this section, we're going to go through a very detailed

series of questions that will give you a clear idea of who you should be targeting for your cold traffic campaigns.

The first question you need to answer is: where can you sell your product or service? If you sell physical services, maybe that's a 10-mile radius of your location. Or if you sell physical products, maybe you can sell them nation-wide. If you are selling information products, or consulting, you can sell worldwide if you want to. It's just important to identify any geographical limitations, because location is a big part of effective targeting If you are in a brick-and-mortar business, or a location-dependent business, you don't need to rely so much on interest targeting.

Unless you're in a huge city, your audience size is going to be small, and what's unique about them is the town or city they live in. A good rule of thumb is that if you're living in a location with less than 300,000 people, you can just use the location targeting and maybe one big overlay interest or data point. For example, I had a student targeting women who had recently gotten engaged in a small city, and she just targeted her ads to women in that location who had recently added interest points to their profile around being engaged or getting married. As long as the audience size doesn't drop below 5000 or so, you're good to go.

After you've established your location setting, there are three different categories I think about when I'm targeting a new avatar or market. If you can answer at least some of the questions from each of these categories, you'll be able to start targeting your cold traffic very effectively.

Category #1: Product and Service Consumption

What else are they buying, and from whom, in your market? Back to the yoga example, what other items, products or services is that passionate yogi purchasing in your market?

- Which "tools" does your avatar use in your market? (for yogis, this might be yoga mats, blocks, straps, yoga clothing, incense, blankets and so on.)
- Which brands makes those tools?
- Which online stores does your avatar shop in?
- Which physical stores do they shop in?
- Who are your competitors?
- What apps is your avatar using? (This can be a good indicator of interests one step removed from your product. For example, a lot of yogis also meditate, so you could target the audience of meditation apps.)
- What software is the avatar using?
- What else are they buying in your market?
- Which brands make those products/services?

CATEGORY #2: COMMUNITY AND CONGREGATION

Are there communities in your market? Do they congregate anywhere online or offline?

Most people will be able to say yes to these questions, even if you're selling commodity products — for example, if you are selling toothbrushes, and one of your avatars is a mom, you can ask yourself if moms congregate anywhere online or offline. Heck yes they do! They congregate in a lot of places and different ways. If someone cares enough about this interest to turn up to an event or location, they are highly likely to be part of that core, avid part of the market.

- What live events does your avatar attend? (Conferences, tournaments, seminars, pop-events, parties)

- What online events does your avatar attend? (Webinars, training calls, live social media broadcasts)
- What online forums, message boards or groups are they using to engage with this interest?
- What associations are they a part of?
- What clubs are they a part of?
- What buzzwords or keywords does your avatar use — what do they talk a lot about? (This is important because some of those keywords might be listed as interests in Facebook)

CATEGORY #3: CONTENT CONSUMPTION

Is your avatar consuming content about your market topic? If yes, in what medium, and from whom?

- Which blogs do they read?
- Which books do they read?
- Which magazines do they read?
- Which TV shows do they watch?
- Which movies do they watch?
- Which podcasts do they listen to?
- Which social media accounts do they follow (for entertainment or education)?
- Which influencers, educators, entertainers, celebrities, and influential people are they following in your market (who else has your market's attention)?

All these categories give you so much more depth in how you're able to connect with your market. There's so much more emotion and empathy you can bring to your avatar when you really understand their experiences and worldview.

And if you sell commodity items (or specialty items, for that matter) you can also use triggering events in your targeting. Triggering events create windows of opportunity, where your prospect is far more likely to act — these are things that happen in your avatar's life that make them more open to your offer than usual. Think about what type of event would trigger the need or desire in your avatar to buy from you. Some big, very common examples of triggering events include:

- Change of job
- Discovery of pregnancy
- Birth of a child
- Engagement
- Marriage
- Divorce
- Birthday
- Anniversary
- Holiday
- Graduating
- Aging
- Death of a loved one
- Major system failure (like air conditioning breaking in summer, or a CRM crashing mid-launch)

These events are less about *who* the avatar is and more about what they're currently experiencing that makes your offer relevant to them. This is one of the few times I'll go into the dropdown interest menus in the Facebook ads manager to go through all the Life Events targeting options.

Work through each of these categories for each of the different avatars you are going to target with your campaign. Remember that you should have a different ad campaign targeting each different avatar, so that you're not trying to create campaigns that speak to all different types of people. It might take you an hour to work through that list, or it might take you a day, but I recommend working through it with pen and paper, based on your own experience with the market and researching every question on Google, Amazon and Facebook to see what else you can find.

Once you've answered all those questions for your avatar, you can switch over to the Facebook ads manager and start interest matching — cross-referencing all the answers on your list with the interests available for targeting. Go to the Detailed Interests field and type in the name or keyword and see if a dropdown appears. If it does, it will show you the number of people Facebook has tagged with that interest. For example, Chase Jarvis, an authority figure who showed up in my research for the photography space, is an interest point for 154,000 people on Facebook. You then write down that number next to the name or keyword in your notes, and continue to cross-reference the rest of your list. If one of your notes doesn't have a dropdown or any number associated with it, remove it from your list.

As a general rule, each of your ad sets should target audience sizes between 500,000 people and 3 to 5 million people when testing, and 30 to 60 million when scaling (though if you're a local business, those numbers can be a lot smaller, particularly in small locations). This seems to be the sweet spot where Facebook can really optimize the campaigns. Aiming for an audience of this size obviously means that you won't be able to target every single interest that showed up, so you will need to sort through all the avatar data you collected earlier to select the handful of interests you're going to focus on. You can also click through to Audience Insights to see which Facebook pages these interest pages have liked to give yourself some more data to work with.

When I'm selecting these interests specifically for each ad set, I like to prioritize brands and very specific interests that only the avid core of the market would engage with. Once you've selected a set of interests that takes your total audience to that ideal range of between 500,000 and 3 to 5 million, you can move onto the next stage of building that ad set. I will usually build three ad sets per campaign, varying the interests I target and the audience sizes, to get a feel for what works best for this avatar.

AD SCENT

The last important thing to consider when setting up ad campaigns is the user experience of the ad, also known as ad scent. This is the relationship between the ads that you're running and the page that traffic is landing on, and how congruent that experience is for the end user at each new stage. Whenever you send traffic to a landing page, it should look and feel congruent with the ad.

Think about how your ad and landing page will work together from a prospect's perspective, and make sure it's a seamless process for them to move through each next step. The reason people clicked is the 'why' you showed them in the ad — the transformation opportunity is going to be what got their attention. It's key to continue that message onto the next page to keep their attention and to continue building trust with them.

Let's say, for example, that you're sending traffic to an opt-in page where you're asking people for their email address, and that 25% of the people that land on that page subscribe, with a cost per lead of $2. That means you're *losing*

75% of your traffic. To optimize that campaign, most people would make changes to their traffic campaign, which is reasonable, but they forget to think about the page the user is landing on, and often this is actually where the problem lies. If they changed the on-page experience to be more congruent and more focused on the prospect's experience (instead of changing the traffic source), they could feasibly double that opt-in rate and take it to 50%, which would mean that the cost per lead would immediately be cut in half and go down to $1.

The core part of ad scent comes from the idea that we all browse the Internet in a hub and spoke model — we're all searching for something. Even if you're on Facebook mindlessly scrolling, your brain is on a hunt, which is why you can be scrolling through Facebook and look up and suddenly realize 20 minutes have gone by without you even noticing. It's because everything that you were doing was congruent — you weren't seeing anything unexpected, everything was very consistent.

In that situation, it's only when there is a point of incongruence in your experience that you hit the back button or close the tab. Something doesn't line up with your expectations, so it jars you out of your search and makes you switch to something else. As a marketer, you want to make sure you provide the best ad scent possible — the most congruent and consistent experience you possibly can — so that people continue to take the actions you want them to take and don't have any jarring moments that put them off.

An inconsistency that makes people drop off when they click through from an ad can really hurt your campaigns. There are a few elements that are important for maintaining this consistency so that your campaigns do as well as possible.

The first is design — it's great if you can use similar

imagery between your ad creative and your landing page. If you have a video in your ad, you can use that same video on the landing page. Whatever you're using in terms of imagery in your ads (including color scheme, typeface and layout) should be mirrored on your landing page. Most media buyers do not design the pages they send traffic to, and this is why it's so important to be able to communicate well with your designers.

The second is copy and messaging. Use very similar copy on your landing page to what is in your ads, because if someone aligns with your ad copy and sees consistent messaging when they click over to the landing page, they're going to continue forward. I often write the landing page copy first, and then use that same copy in my ads to ensure there's no big difference in what prospects are reading at each stage.

And finally, your offer should be consistent! Don't try to 'bait-and-switch' people. It's shocking how often this happens. I've seen a dentist offering free teeth-whitening in the ad, but when you click over to the landing page there's just an opt-in form with no mention of that free teeth-whitening. I've even seen big movie studios do this. I saw an ad for a free four-day, three-night vacation with one of the biggest studios in the world, and when I clicked over to the landing page, there were a ton of packages I could buy, but no mention of the deal that they had offered in the ad. That's really confusing and jarring for the user, and mistakes like this just drive leads away.

Another reason ad scent is important is that advertising platforms like Facebook and Google Adwords are monitoring how many people click on your ad, and then how much time they spend on the next page. How many of them close the tab or hit the back button very quickly? That shows Google or Facebook that even though the ad might have a high click-through rate, the experience the advertiser is providing on the next page is not congruent, so the algorithm should dial down the reach this ad is getting.

And this isn't just in media buying — consistency is key throughout marketing in general, so make sure you always step back and look at the bird's eye view of the entire customer experience when you're running campaigns.

11

A DAY IN THE LIFE OF A MEDIA BUYER

What does a day in the life of a media buyer look like? I've mapped out a typical day for an in-house media buyer here to give you an idea, though this will also apply if you're working with multiple clients. Some aspects of this 'typical day' will vary by the business and its size, but you can tweak the variables in this formula to find the result that works best for you. This schedule is not designed to be prescriptive — it's intended to illustrate what a media buyer should be focusing on, and for how long, so that you can get the best results.

The devil is in the details, as they say, and that's very true in this field. Media buying is a process of iteration, of continually optimizing and spending every day making each campaign better. That's really fun, because there's always something to do — coming up with new ideas for ads, fine-tuning your targeting and so on. In this chapter you're going to see exactly how the system works, how the maintenance works, how the optimization works — what I do step by step every day to get amazing results for my projects.

SCHEDULE OVERVIEW

8:30am — 9:00am: Get settled & check campaign stats

This is really simple, and really important. This is the information that will tell you what to turn off, what to scale, what needs more work, and it makes sure you know if there are any fires that need to be put out. It acts as the scoreboard for where all your campaigns stand each day.

9:00 — 9:30am: Turn off under-performers & scale budgets

It seems easier for Facebook to apply things like budget increases when they're done in the morning. If you scale at night, it won't damage your campaign, but Facebook won't have time to fully scale that increase in the short period of time before you come back to check the results the next morning.

9:45 — 10:45am: Building new ads or strategy

This is the best timing for me to do this, because I'm most energetic and clear-headed in the morning. By the afternoon I'm often a little brain-foggy, so I always like to put build time in the morning. It's usually an hour a day for me, though that will vary a lot based on how many campaigns you're running.

This hour is for building new campaigns and coming up with new ad strategies. It's also great because if you're going to launch a new campaign, it can be done earlier in the morning, versus later in the day, which again gives Facebook time to optimize that campaign's distribution before you come back to check it.

. . .

11:00am — 12:00pm: Targeting research

The people I see succeed the most in this field are the ones that are willing to go deep on their targeting research, to really get into the psychology of their market and do the research on where those people can be found. An hour might seem like a long time to spend on this, but as you found in the last chapter, there's a lot of complexity in targeting, so an hour is really not much.

12:00pm — 1:00pm: Lunch!

Remember: you have to take care of yourself to get the best results in your work, so take a proper break. Go for a walk, eat some healthy food, connect with someone in the real world.

1:00pm — 2:30pm: Team/company meetings

Again, this will depend on your company's size and set-up, but early afternoons have always worked well for me to do meetings. Whether that's client meetings or team meetings, it allows you to have your creative time in the morning, but media buyers are nothing without collaboration. Even though ads can have a huge effect on a business, they only work when the the offer is right, the design is great, the copy resonates, if the tracking is there, the tech is right and the customer service is ready. You really need to integrate yourself with the rest of the company to have the best chance of success.

2:45pm — 4:00pm: Creative and/or copy focus

If you decided in the morning that you needed to develop a new strategy for ads, I've found that the afternoon is a great time for me to do that. This is especially important when it comes to creative — many media buyers don't give their designers enough instruction on the creative, and end up with very pretty ads that don't work, so this is the window to get with your designer to make sure the ads you're working on together are going to convert.

4:15pm — 5:00pm: Ad research & education time

Facebook literally changes every day, so while my job is to run Facebook ads, it's also my job to be a Facebook detective. I don't want to encourage shiny object syndrome, but you do need to know about changes that are coming. So at this time I read up on any new developments, look at what other brands are doing, and update my processes to account for any changes.

5:00 — 5:30: Check campaign stats & plan next day

Last but not least, check your campaign stats before you leave, just to make sure you jump on any big opportunities that have emerged since you tweaked everything in the morning, and then plan your next day. Then go home! Get some rest and come back fresh tomorrow.

SCHEDULE DEEP DIVE

So now that you have a sense of how the day typically unfolds, let's look at each of those pieces in more depth. It's all very well to tell you what to do, but you also need to understand how and why each of these pieces happen.

CHECKING CAMPAIGN STATS

Before you check your stats, you first have to know what your success metrics are. This is a huge mistake that happens a lot: the media buyer sets up campaigns, starts running all this traffic, *before* everyone in the company has gotten aligned on what a good campaign is and what a bad campaign is.

The success or failure of a campaign should not be a subjective conversation; you have to make sure as the media buyer that you have a clear indication from the business owner or CEO (or whoever you report to) about what they want and what success actually means. And if you're a business owner, you have to be clear with your media buyer about what you want and how you want to track that. There are a bunch of different metrics to track, based on your business model, but some of the most common and impactful metrics to track include:

- Return on ad spend (ROAS): if you put $1 into Facebook, do you make more back?
- Cost per acquisition of a customer (CPA): the amount you have to spend to get someone to buy a product.
- CPL (cost per lead): what it costs to get someone to give you an email address.

You can also measure metrics like:

- Cost per click (CPC): a high CPC might be okay if your CPL is still within reason, but it could also tell you that your ad's relevance score is low.
- Clickthrough rate (CTR): this is a great way to measure if your offer and copy are resonating enough with your audience to make them click.
- Conversion Rate on Page (CR on page): this is

something most people completely forget about until they go to optimize their offer. When they make some tweaks on the landing page that the ad directs traffic to, they might increase their CR on page from 10% to 20%, which cuts their CPA in half.

- Ad relevance diagnostics: these are three metrics that help you diagnose whether the ads you ran were relevant to the audience you reached. Here's what Facebook says about them:

  *"**Quality ranking**: How your ad's perceived quality compared to ads competing for the same audience.*

  ***Engagement rate ranking**: How your ad's expected engagement rate compared to ads competing for the same audience.*

  ***Conversion rate ranking**: How your ad's expected conversion rate compared to ads with the same optimization goal competing for the same audience."*[1]

- Customer experience diagnostics: These are two 'quality assurance' scores. The customer feedback score is Facebook's way of measuring the experience a brand provides to consumers AFTER they purchase. This shows up as a survey in their Facebook feed, asking if they were satisfied with your shipping, product quality, etc. This score populates into a number out of 5: a low score will negatively affect your advertising ability from that brand page. The other score is page quality, which allows Facebook to measure the quality of your Facebook brand page, both from a paid *and*

organic perspective. Under this tab you'll find if
your page has any violations for sharing fake news
or breaking terms of service.

At DigitalMarketer, we tracked our ad campaigns
according to the avatar we were targeting and the 'hook' we
were using to get their attention. I still do something similar
today — I break down all the campaigns so I can quickly
look at each one in a spreadsheet and see what the ROI, CPL
and CPA are. I might also have fields for those secondary
metrics: clicks, opt-ins and total spend.

You don't necessarily have to start your reporting with
something this elaborate — inside Facebook you can
customize the reporting data that is shown to you each day
in their Custom Reports area. Once you have a good idea of
which ads need some assistance and which need to be scaled,
you can then move into a period where you're actually taking
action based off the numbers you have just received.

Turning Off Under-Performers and Scaling Budgets

I like to work with a 'green, yellow, red' traffic light
system as a shorthand to explain how a campaign is
performing. Green means it's doing really well and should be
scaled up. Yellow means it needs some tweaking to perform
better. Red means that it's underperforming and should be
switched off.

In this example, let's say that the goal of the campaign is
to generate leads, and CPL is the primary metric I'm tracking. I want to keep that CPL at or below $1.10, so I set para-
meters that will let me know whether the campaign is green,
yellow or red. Red is any ad set that is costing over $1.10.
Yellow is anything between $0.90 and $1.10, and green is
anything under $0.90. I can look at that color code every day

and get an immediate sense of what needs to happen with that campaign. So when you're thinking about campaigns, ask yourself (and your boss or client) what your primary success metric for the campaign is, and then work out how to create a green-yellow-red schema for tracking that.

Any ad that falls into the green category should be scaled up by 50%, every three to five days. If it falls into yellow, leave it alone — that campaign is still within acceptable parameters, so you should keep running it, but scaling might tip it over into red. If an ad falls into the red zone, turn it off.

(As a side note, the green-yellow-red system works so well because everyone you work with will be able to understand it immediately, and it takes all the emotion out of this process. Media buyers really have to keep a clear head. When you're spending a lot of money on ads — usually someone else's money! — it's a big responsibility and you can't let emotions sway your decisions about how you run a campaign. This system ensures you have a reliable, objective way to measure the performance of each campaign, and protects campaigns from being influenced by anyone's emotions or opinions.)

BUILDING NEW ADS AND STRATEGY

The next hour of the day is all about new creation — whether you need to create new ad sets for a campaign, build a new campaign altogether, or create an entirely fresh strategy — you need to ask yourself what new stuff needs to be built each day, and do it during the part of the day when you're most alert.

Let me give you an example of the kind of thing you might build during this chunk of time. This example comes from a client who created a free nine-day video series that sold physical products throughout the series. It was a simple video funnel, providing free education for nine straight days, selling all the while, which is a great way to sell both physical products and info products. My goal was to drive leads to this funnel for less than $1.10 CPL — the goal was customer acquisition, and the client knew from past campaigns that this was the sweet spot for generating the profitability they wanted.

We ran the ads for two months and ended up with 157,000 leads at $1.08 a piece, which made me so proud. We spent $170,000 on ads, made $237,000 back in immediate revenue, we acquired 1130 new customers, added over 157,000 people to the email list, and grew the retargeting audience by 4 million people (500,000 of those visited the website, and 3.5 million people watched the video ad).

During this hour in the morning, I got the bones of this campaign laid out — mapping out the campaign structure by hand in a notebook. Based on my targeting research, I knew that I could run six identical ads in each ad set, and target each ad set to different interests. That gave me a clear sense of what I needed to build that day — all the ads that would make up each of the ad sets.

Whenever I build a new campaign, I always let it run for three full days without changing anything. You're often going to get false positives and negatives while Facebook is optimizing the ad's distribution, so leave it alone for three days to let it get settled (and make sure you always plan that into your test budget).

TARGETING RESEARCH

This is my absolute favorite part of this whole job. My process for targeting research was laid out in full detail in Chapter 7, where I explained every single step I follow to guarantee that the campaigns I'm building so carefully are actually going to be shown to the people who are going to respond. So many people build awesome campaigns, with great offers and copy and creative, and then drop the ball right at the last minute, when they're defining the targeting for the ads. Apart from your offer, I truly believe that targeting is the most important aspect of any campaign.

During this hour every day, I'm spending time researching new audiences for new ad campaigns. If a campaign already has a lot of 'green' ad sets, then part of this time is going to be focused on finding more people who are most similar to the audiences who are already converting. You can also use this time to target new interests and find look-alike audiences.

TEAM AND CLIENT MEETINGS

In this role, it's very important to understand how the role of media buyer relates to the rest of the organization. The media buyer cannot be an island, operating independently. If the media buyer is not fully informed of what's going on in the rest of the company, it can create a lot of problems — you can end up putting the wrong product out, using the wrong messaging, or adding a whole lot of additional pressure to a system that's not working well. The media buyer must relay information and data back to the rest of the team for optimization — for example, if a particular avatar is responding well to a specific type of campaign, that can inform the types of products and offers that are developed in the future. The client or company is of course buying leads and customers through their media campaigns, but they are also buying data about their audience. Whether the media buyer is a consultant or in-house employee, it's important for them to keep in touch with everyone, from the designers to the customer support team. Here are a few key relationships to maintain, and conversations to keep open:

- Customer service: send links to the campaigns to the customer service team (if applicable to your business), so that the customer service reps can respond to questions and comments beneath the ads.
- Data and analysis: if there's a data person on the team, they should be kept in the loop about how the campaigns are performing.
- Tracking: this is about reporting all the numbers in a clear way. Not all media buyers will be great at this but it's important to work through these with the leadership of the business.
- Tech: If something breaks, often the media buyer will be the first to know, so they need to communicate it to the relevant person on the team to get it fixed.
- Promotions: If the business is running promotions or flash sales, the media buyer should know! This is one of the most underutilized types of ads — running traffic to your warm and hot audiences to let them know about this opportunity to buy again.
- Design: media buyers are not designers, and they often need a professional to work with them on ad creative. Even if you don't have a full-time designer, you can use a service like Design Pickle to make sure you're getting professional assets for your campaigns as needed.
- Inventory: if a media buyer sells twice as much inventory as is available, the company is going to run into a whole host of customer service and fulfillment issues, so this is a really important area

to communicate about regularly. Facebook is really focusing now on the quality of customer experiences, so you want to make sure that your campaigns are only scaled to the point that customers continue to have a good experience with your brand.

CREATIVE AND COPY FOCUS

Building the creative and copy assets that your campaigns need can go a couple of ways. Either the media buyer will write all the copy themselves, they'll work with a copywriter if there's one in-house, or the copy can be outsourced to a freelancer or outside partner. Usually the creative elements — the actual design of the images that go with the ads — are left to a designer (either in-house or external), since this is a very different skillset. While there's plenty of opportunity now to create great visuals just using your phone camera, if you can't nail a photo, having a designer on hand is extremely helpful. Remember that your creative and copy are the visual representations of your hook, which help convince your audience that they should opt in to your offer, download your lead magnet or engage with your pre-sale article.

So many media buyers get tired by this stage. When you're setting up a campaign, the copy and creative are the last things to happen, so often people just throw up ads that just list a bunch of features about the product, without tailoring the presentation to the actual avatar... and it just doesn't work. Ads only work when they speak to the end user, when you've taken the time to think about who you are marketing to, and why they will care.

Another issue is that people are not creating enough new ads. They scale their budgets vertically, but not horizontally, and their ads get fatigued. This is a big issue in ad campaigns — the return on an ad will eventually start to decline, because the ad has reached everyone in the audience segment it was targeting. Refreshing the copy and creative helps overcome ad fatigue when you take an ad to a new audience segment.

Remember that your designer is an artist, not a marketer, so they should be open to direction from you, and they should be focused on producing the highest-converting design, not the prettiest pictures.

Years ago at DigitalMarketer, when I first started working with my designer, I would send her the ad copy and ask her to send me a few creative ideas. I would get stuff that was pretty, but it didn't work very well, and so I realized that I needed to give her a lot more direction. A lot of my afternoons ended up focused on developing a creative brief that would give her ideas to develop that would be more aligned with what I had in mind for the ad.

I would go over to Google Images and type in some keywords, so that I could get a feel for what images people were associating with those terms, and then sketch out a few images with some notes about each idea. I would sometimes include screenshots of ads from other brands that could be good inspiration, and I would also include a link to the landing page the ad would direct traffic to, so that she could design creative that would be consistent with the rest of the imagery the audience would see.

I always also asked her to include one 'wildcard' design that was her own idea, and over time, these wildcards have performed better and better as she's gotten better at recognizing what resonates with our audiences. We still work together, and a lot of her wildcards beat my concepts now! But I still send these documents, so that every time we start a new project, she knows exactly what she needs to create.

. . .

AD RESEARCH AND EDUCATION

I get a lot of ideas for creative, copy and hooks by looking at what other brands are doing, usually outside of the market I'm working in. Media buying is not all clicking buttons and setting up tracking — you have to give yourself time to do research, to get inspiration and let your creativity come out. It's okay to look at what other marketers are doing, to adapt great ideas for your own campaigns and to learn from what other people are having success with. I build 'swipe files' (screenshots and analysis) of interesting or innovative campaigns I can use to get my creative juices flowing when I'm working on a new campaign. (All this is available in the Facebook Ads Library, and you can also grab a curated collection of great ads I put together into an Adsumer Report at mollypittman.com/clickhappy.)

The landscape for media buying changes very fast, so you do have to put in some work to stay up to date. The end of the day is a great time to go through a course, listen to a podcast, read some new blog posts and so on. There are so many people out there teaching what's working, so if you're the media buyer, make sure you're absorbing that material regularly to make sure you stay competitive (and if you're hiring a media buyer, ask them about who they follow to keep up to date).

You cannot be in this business and refuse to continue your education — I am still learning new things every single day. Continuing to work on your skills and knowledge of the platform is just as important as all the other metrics you work towards, because if you don't do this, your knowledge will quickly become outdated and your campaigns will quickly suffer.

. . .

FINAL CAMPAIGN CHECK AND NEXT-DAY PLANNING

At the very end of the day, you want to quickly check on your campaigns to make sure everything is in good shape, and whether there are any campaigns you have the opportunity to scale before you leave. Then plan the following day — I'm always much more successful when I have laid out my day the night before. Think about whether any of the ad copy or creative you worked on today is going to be ready to launch tomorrow. Do you see any 'yellow' campaigns fatiguing that might need some attention? Are there any new launches or offers rolling out from the business in the next few days or weeks that you need to plan for? Are you keeping up and hitting your goals and metrics?

And if you're wondering how you scale a campaign, let me explain what I did with the earlier example. First, I let the campaign run for the initial three days while Facebook optimized the ad distribution. After those three days, and every morning thereafter, I turned off any ad sets there were above the 'red' $1.10 CPL mark we had set as the upper limit. Every three days, I increased the budget of ad sets that were below the 'green' $0.90 CPL by 50% (which I call vertical scaling). Every three days I also created a new ad set with new targeting (which I call horizontal scaling).

Keep in mind that a small number of your ad sets will deliver the biggest result. This is really common — it's known as the 80/20 rule, which says that 80% of your results will come from 20% of your effort. That means that you can just focus on scaling the ads that are obviously outperforming the rest, and ignore the rest.

And you should know that 30 to 40% of my ads fail immediately. I'm pretty darn good at this stuff, but even so, the failure rate on paid media is always high. If all your campaigns are perfect, it's a sign you're not pushing yourself hard enough — media buying is competitive, and you need to try new things to the point that you're failing sometimes, or you're not maximising on the opportunities in front of you.

Once you've scaled anything obvious and planned your day, make sure you disconnect and enjoy your evening. Most of my good ideas come to me when I'm not 'working' — when I'm outside, or talking to a friend, or doing something creative — and my brain is relaxed enough to come up with that idea that I've been trying to pin down for days.

THRIVING IN THE DIGITAL ERA

Working in the digital economy is one of the biggest opportunities in the world today. Media buying in particular has very high leverage, because it gives you the ability to quickly grow and monetize a business — and it's all trackable. You can demonstrate your value to clients almost immediately, and as a result, you become indispensable to the business. But before you can do this, there are a few practical things you need to know. In this chapter, I want to give you some really hands-on insights to help you get on your way finding your place in digital.

COMPENSATION

If you want to work as an in-house media buyer, or with a single client, expect to be paid a base salary. An entry-level package will usually be in the region of $50,000 (USD). But after you start to consistently generate results, after six to twelve months, or if you already have experience and expertise, then you can consider a different compensation model.

There are a lot of different ways to do that, but I think the best option for an in-house media buyer is a percentage of top-line revenue. It aligns your incentives with that of the business — the more revenue generated, the more money everybody makes. This is usually a better option than other percentage-share arrangements, which tend to get messy (because cross-platform tracking isn't perfect). Some companies offer a percentage of profit, but this can be a bad deal for media buyers, because profit is affected by many things. For example, if the owner decides to double the cost of the product to improve quality, that's their decision, but it will mean a change in the total profit of the business, and it's not fair if your income is affected by that.

For the freelancer or agency owner, the most effective arrangement tends to be a monthly retainer and an additional performance-based fee. Normally this is arranged on cost per acquisition, meaning that the client pays you a fixed amount for every lead you drive or every customer that you bring in. Most clients won't feel confident giving away a percentage of top line revenue to an external partner (unless you're very experienced and have proven yourself to be extremely trustworthy and valuable).

PROFESSIONAL GROWTH

When you're just starting out, you need to build your foundational knowledge. That's everything from knowing the language a media buyer uses, the metrics they should track, how to set up a campaign, and you can get most of this knowledge from courses and mentorships like Train My Traffic Person, the course I run with Ezra Firestone to teach new media buyers everything they need to know.

The second element here is experience. There's nothing that will teach you more about media buying than getting your own experience. Even a failed campaign has so much valuable data and information, and it will make you a better media buyer. Keep in mind that even very experienced media buyers have huge failure rates on their campaigns. Even now, only about 20% of the campaigns I run are 'successful' — a full 80% of my campaigns don't work. Those 20% are successful enough that they make up for the 80% that don't, and every campaign teaches me something new that makes me better for the next one. Learning on the job like this is where most of your learning is going to come from.

Finally, you need ongoing education. It's why Ezra and I also have Team Traffic, a monthly coaching program for media buyers. In that program, we aggregate all the updated information from Facebook each month, share analysis of what that means for our members, and share insights into what is working right now. This stuff changes so much, all the time — a lot of our ongoing education is just about keeping up with what's happening in the industry. Going to events, talking to other media buyers, and listening to podcasts and webinars will also help you keep up to date.

Media buying lends itself to a collaborative dynamic within the industry, rather than an aggressively competitive dynamic. Anyone in media buying who is holding secrets close to their chest is most probably suffering from a scarcity mindset, but we all do better when we share what's working and what's not. And it's so important to have peers in media buying that you can talk to when something isn't working, when you've discovered something cool or when you have something to celebrate. When your relevance score jumps to a 10 from a 5, your friends outside the industry might be pleased for you that something is working, but your media buyer friends will be so excited *with* you, because they understand why that's so significant.

While I've been careful to build friendships outside the industry in recent years, much of my success has come from the abundance of working with friends in this industry. There is space in the market for all of us. Some of my best friends are running ads in the same markets that I am, and that makes me excited, because that creates so much more knowledge and experience we can all share. If five of us are working in the market, that's five times the knowledge I could build about this market on my own.

I really appreciate that my career started at DigitalMarketer, because a big part of my role was passing knowledge along — our business model was built around teaching what we found — and so from the start I was trained to share everything so that everyone benefits. This is why I love events teaching at events, sharing on podcasts and being in Facebook groups with other media buyers — the more we share and learn, the better advertising and the better the consumer experience will be. It creates a virtuous cycle.

MANAGING YOUR SCHEDULE AND DEALING WITH CLIENTS

When I struck out on my own, I was looking for freedom, and the ability to work on what I wanted, when I wanted. So while I knew I needed to pay the bills and start generating momentum for my new solo business, I didn't give myself any structure... and while it was amazing to feel like I didn't have to stick to anyone's agenda, the lack of structure turned out to be a mistake. It became extremely difficult to manage all my new work without a clear plan, and so working independently ended up feeling overwhelming and stressful, rather than fun and flexible.

After the first few months, I started keeping a notebook with a little box for each client that had a list of things I needed to work on next for them, and when I was going to speak to them next. I decided that I would do all my calls —

recurring client calls, sales meetings, recording interviews — on Tuesdays and Wednesdays, so that I would have at least three days each week where I would actually do the work for each client, since it might take anywhere from five and fifteen hours to develop a new campaign, depending on the complexity. Learning to manage my time and workflow really paved the way for me to start feeling more comfortable away from the traditional structure of a job. Now the work does feel fun and flexible, because I know all my responsibilities are planned for and I can choose how to use my time to get them all done in a way that works for me personally.

When you're freelancing or looking to take on clients, you definitely have to consider how you're going to manage your time and your boundaries. Having a healthy relationship with clients often comes down to setting clear expectations at the start of each project. There are a few simple things you can do to make sure things stay organized and that their expectations align with your plan. Let them know:

- Roughly how long the project should take.
- How they should contact you (pick a single channel, and have them stick to it — either email, a messaging app, or a project management tool) and in what timeframe they can expect a reply.
- How they can raise ideas, concerns or changes with you.
- The exact deliverables of the project, and what happens if the scope of the project changes (such as fees for delays on their part or pricing for additional requests).
- Where all the documentation and assets will be kept and managed.
- Introduce them to any team members or contractors that will be helping you.

This wasn't something I was great at to begin with. If you don't set firm boundaries, your work will creep into your whole life. Clients will send you an email, and if they don't hear back straight away, they'll text you, send a Facebook message, and try to call. It's not that they're trying to annoy you or be difficult — it's usually because they're anxious about something or have an idea to share.

Setting expectations and establishing boundaries prevents (or least minimizes) this 'communication creep' — they can feel confident that you're going to handle things, because you've told them how and when that's going to happen. This also ensures that the client understands the full value of your services, because their expectation of what you're going to deliver matches what you plan to deliver. Not only do you need to lay out how the relationship is going to work, you need to set the expectations of the work you're going to do and the results you're going to deliver.

Even now, when I'm teaching courses that have a coaching component, I'll let students know to give me 24 to 48 hours to respond to them. If they submit material for critiques, I'll cover it on our next group call, and if we run out of time there, I'll shoot a video to answer their questions. They know exactly when to expect feedback, and setting these expectations from the start establishes a dynamic where everyone feels like their needs are being met and their time is being respected.

Here are some questions to help you work out what these boundaries are for you:

- How do you want clients to communicate with you?
- What kind of response time do you think is reasonable?
- What are the deliverables for each project?

- Where and how do you want to manage each project?
- How often will you give them updates, and how will that happen?
- What results can they expect from you?

You can set these expectations in your sales calls, in your contracts, in your onboarding packages — there are multiple opportunities to establish a healthy relationship, before the work even starts. (And if someone pushes back on your boundaries from the start, you have an opportunity to decide if you want to go ahead with their project — if they can't respect simple guidelines from the beginning, they're not going to respect what you ask of them later on either.)

You've probably heard the saying that 'the customer is always right'. This is not always true, and this idea gets a lot of freelancers and consultants into trouble. It's understandable that you would want to make all your clients happy — you worry that if you disagree with someone, or do something different to how they want it done, then they won't pay you, or they'll say bad things about you in the industry. But you're the expert in this relationship, so this is a question of setting expectations about the dynamic of the partnership. Both parties are equally important in client-consultant relationships, and give each other an equal amount of value, so it's really important for you to establish a partnership dynamic, rather than a boss-employee dynamic.

You have to establish the conditions of your relationship so that everybody ends up happy with the outcomes. Both parties have to agree on what success looks like, regardless of how many times you have calls, or how many hours you log working on the project. That could be results-based ('I'm going to deliver 1000 leads for you every month') or deliverable-based ('I'm going to set up an ad campaign for you every month'). This agreement should be reinforced and reported on every week or month to make sure you are demonstrating the value you are giving them. It's up to you to communicate how you're meeting those expectations. The great thing about this is that you will be able to see, objectively, when you've done the work you agreed to, to the standard you agreed to. You can both immediately see when a good job has been done, which frees you up from wondering if you've done a good job or whether the client is happy.

Sometimes even the best plans go sideways. Someone forgets to send an asset, a campaign doesn't work, someone misses an important call — these things happen. Sometimes it will be on you (you get sick, something goes wrong in your personal life, you make a mistake), and sometimes it will be on them (something in the rest of the marketing is causing problems in the campaign, something goes wrong in *their* personal life or team, and so on). No matter whose side the issue is on, you need to be able to lead that conversation in an open and calm way to get it resolved.

If you are consistently communicating with the client, then none of these things should become a big deal. If you are sending a weekly report with the data that shows how you've performed, based on the goals you set together, then you already have a line of communication open to address anything that's getting out of whack. You just have to be able to be upfront and honest about what's going on.

PRIORITIZING YOUR PERSONAL LIFE

I love the idea of scheduling everything that's a priority for you, *before* you schedule your work — time with your family, working out, maintaining hobbies and so on. If you don't, there will always be something 'more important' that comes up on the job and the other key areas of your life will suffer.

We work to live — not the other way around — and you have to actively prioritize the things in your life that are *not* work. For most of us, work will expand to take up all the time that we make available. It's easy to forget to make time for *living* and doing the things that keep you happy and healthy.

This is partly because communication is instantaneous these days, and because in our culture, 'busy' means 'successful.' Remember that someone else's urgency is not your urgency. It's super common that someone will come to you with something they consider very urgent, and try to place that stress on you — via an email or text message or a call — to get it done right now.

But urgent and important are not the same thing, and you are not at the beck and call of everyone in your life. Yes, there will be situations that need to be dealt with quickly, but often, it can wait. It's up to you to use your judgement, and when you choose to set a boundary, to enforce it so that you're not in a constant place of stress and anxiety responding to things you don't value.

I'm not saying this easy. It can be very hard and it takes practice to differentiate between what's truly urgent and what can wait just a little bit longer. But thriving in digital is about learning to manage your energy and working on the right thing at the right time.

Now, you might be reading this and thinking, "Molly, that sounds nice and all — but I just quit my job! I've got to pay my rent and I'd like to eat today; how can I possibly push back on someone who's going to pay my bills?!"

True, when you're in that early time of working for yourself, you are definitely going to have a lot more urgency riding on all the work you're doing. It probably *is* going to be more stressful, but my best piece of advice is to trust: trust the universe, trust yourself, trust that this is going to work out.

Don't make any rash decisions that are going to get you into a place with a client that really stresses you out, or where you can't step away from the work for a single moment to stop everything from crashing down.

Don't make decisions based on fear about money. I definitely made that mistake, I said yes to *everything* for the first few months I was out on my own, even when I knew deep down that a client or project was not going to be good for me. In hindsight, I'm glad I did, because it helped me learn all the lessons in this book, but I did it because I was so worried about money, and I didn't need to be.

Given that you left your job or started your new business because you want to be happier, less stressed and more in control of your time, don't let fear get the better of you. Don't let it push you into new situations where you're unhappy, stressed and not in control of your time — all without the upside of a regular job's security. That's a *worse* position to be in, not better, so trust that the right things are going to come along for you, and spend your time seeking them out, rather than working on stuff that doesn't serve you.

Finally, understand that life is very seasonal. There will be times when things are more stressful and urgent than at other times — it's not realistic to think that every day from now on is going to be a blissful balance of work you love and a perfectly happy and peaceful personal life. When you're in those moments of stress, the most important thing is to focus on what needs to be prioritized, and what needs to happen to move yourself to the next level of where you want to be. Remember that things will change. Even though I was stressed in those early months of my business, I knew that a year in, I would be in a much better place, and now I am.

You're only going to start out on this journey for the first time once, and saying no to things you know are wrong for you will leave space for things that will be right. The concept of leaving space for yourself to figure stuff out is really important. If every moment of your day is accounted for, there's no breathing room for thinking or growing. You need time to think, to meditate, to connect with your mission, so that you can get clarity on what you're working towards and what your next moves need to be.

Allowing for that space is much more important than being as productive as you possibly can be every day — because ultimately, giving yourself time to think will help you avoid working on things that stunt your progress or throw you off course. That clarity will help you identify the clients and projects that are going to be most successful and most fulfilling for you.

MARKETING YOURSELF

Marketing yourself is a must when you go out on your own. The first step in building up your marketing is to get some results for clients. The best place to start for that is with existing relationships, or working with local businesses that you can approach with a really risk-free offer. I started in a different way to what most people will experience — I fell into this through an internship I found on Craigslist! — and I was able to generate a lot of my authority from an audience that DigitalMarketer had already built.

Most people won't have that, so I recommend doing what Mackensie Liberman did. Mackensie was a cytogeneticist, researching chromosomes after studying biology. She decided that she needed more flexibility in her life, so she asked a restaurant where she ate regularly to take a shot on her — they didn't have to pay her, but if they would give her a monthly budget of $500, she would try to bring them some new customers with Facebook ads. She set up a really simple funnel, targeting people in her town, giving people a coupon for the restaurant when it was their birthday. It worked really well, and they brought in a bunch of new customers. The restaurant ended up paying her monthly, and she was able to take this case study to approach other people to become clients. Just try to get some results. Even if you have to give your services away for free, that's totally fine. All you need is a couple of case studies to show that you can deliver, and you'll be on your way.

Then you need to start to build a social media presence. That might be writing about what you're doing, sharing posts about your work and life, or whatever feels natural for you to start building up. I wish I would have started this much earlier — when I started really working on it, within six weeks my following on Instagram increased to about 5000 people, and 30,000 likes on my Facebook page. That might not seem like a big deal, but people pass a lot of judgement on your position by your social followings. If a client is considering hiring you, they want to be able to Google you, to search Facebook or Instagram or LinkedIn and at least be able to find you and see that you're a real person. It's not just a client acquisition tool; it also adds trust and credibility.

Any way that you can display your knowledge and your skills, the more authority you're going to have. That's why starting the Perpetual Traffic Podcast was one of the best things I've ever done — people can go listen to that podcast and actually start to understand what I'm talking about. Not only do they get value, but they don't have to quiz me as much when we get on the phone. They already know and trust me, because they've heard me talk about my expertise in so much depth. By the time we get on the phone, they're like, "Yes! I know you know your stuff, I wanna hire you, let's do this!" Building these big authority assets (like creating a podcast, writing a book, or creating a course) might come later on once you've got a proven expertise and system, but displaying your knowledge publicly can build a business from the ground up.

Finally, use the skills you're developing as a media buyer to generate more clients for yourself. Practice on your own business. Maybe you turn one of your case studies into a lead magnet that you can exchange for someone's email address or phone number, so you have the ability to follow up and see if they would be a good fit as a client. You could build a webinar where you teach something valuable before you pitch them on your services. Develop relationships with other agency owners — there are lots of different types of agencies, serving lots of different businesses, in lots of different stages of growth.

MANAGING YOUR MONEY AND YOUR GROWTH

James Schramko is my business coach and has had a big influence on my success. He is the host of the SuperFast Business Podcast and an amazing entrepreneurial coach. His book, *Work Less, Make More*, is focused on helping entrepreneurs, freelancers and business owners to get their work-life balance under control by calculating one key metric that will improve everything else.

James was kind enough to give me some of his time to talk about this concept, and to lay out a process that will enable you to build an effective, profitable, fun business around the skills in this book. He has been incredibly successful, and has an amazing work-life balance. He surfs a couple of hours every day, spends lots of time with his family, and has been able to scale and automate his business massively with the approach he's going to share here. Even if you're working for someone else, or haven't yet started your own thing, this is an incredibly valuable insight into the mechanics of building a successful business, so let's jump in:

 To work less and make more, all you need to do is move the needle on one one metric: Effective Hourly Rate (EHR).

Here's how you calculate your EHR:

1. Take the amount of revenue you make in a month and subtract your costs. What you have left is your monthly profit. (If you have a job, them your wage is your profit.)

2. Divide your profit by the number of hours you worked in the month to get it. The number you have now is your EHR.

When I was the general manager of a car dealership, my EHR was much higher than many other employees in the company. I realized I should only be doing really high-value tasks to justify that high wage, instead of wasting any time on tasks that could be handled by someone with a lower EHR, like an admin assistant or sales associate.

Years later, as I built my own business, I ended up with multiple different income streams, and had to have a Battle Royale between my own business units to choose which ones to focus on. I needed a tool to choose where to put my attention, so I started mapping the EHR across each of the different divisions: how much money do I make from this division? What are the costs? How many hours do I put into it? There were secondary considerations too — is there an asset-value being created? Is this feeding some other part of the business? Do I love it? Ultimately, EHR was a very effective way of measuring where I was wasting time and where it was paying off. Things like doing customer support, editing my podcast and booking travel couldn't survive the EHR filter, so it forced me to either hire someone or to get rid of the task altogether.

If you're just starting out, you can maximize your EHR by cutting back on things that you know are completely unproductive (social media, watching videos and checking email are all huge time-sucks).

And if you're in panic mode because you don't know where your next paycheck is coming from, and you want to say yes to everything just to see what works, start scoring each task. If you can at least develop a theory about what the EHR will be of each potential project, you will save yourself some mistakes in advance.

A wage is an EHR — you always make the same amount for each hour you work. But in a less tangible situation, such as running a media agency, think about how many hours you will spend selling your service to the client, how many hours you will need to fulfil that service, how many hours you will spend reporting, and then how much you will earn from that client per month. If you get $3000 from that client, and you spend 100 hours, you're earning $30 per hour. Then you can compare that to another opportunity using the same matrix, and see which one works out better.

A lot of people chase work in markets where there is no money, which is a recipe for frustration. Just because you're good at something, and because people want something for a low price, doesn't mean you have to provide it. I'm really good at polishing shoes, but I'm not going to set up a shoe-shine business. Someone else can fill that gap in the market. If a potential client doesn't meet a minimum threshold, I won't even show them my offer, because it's a waste of my time and theirs — they can't meet the EHR I want to generate and they're not in a position to implement my expertise anyway. There are not many people serving the top of my market (which is true for many markets), and there's not much competition, so I can maximize my EHR by focusing all my effort here.

If you are thinking about starting your own business, aim to make three times as much as you are earning now to make it worthwhile. There will be stress and setbacks, that is 100% guaranteed, so you need to know it will be worth it. There is a phase of business that my mentor described as 'crawling over broken glass' when you first start out. There's no way to get the pay-off without going through that ordeal, but once you do, life is much better, and much easier.

Charge twice as much as you think you

need to charge. You need to have a lot more profit margin than you think. People make the mistake of selling by the hour, which is a hard way to sell any valuable service — it's better to sell by the value of the service to the customer. Be confident in your ability. You've invested in training, you've learned what you need to know, you've practiced and gotten some results, so bank those wins and gradually increase your rates. Charge more than you think you need to, because you're going to have expenses like tax, team, marketing, and don't forget that all real businesses need a healthy profit margin to exist.

To protect yourself right from the start, get paid up front, instead of in arrears. Don't let customers get credit with your business; you're not a bank. I started working this way when I first started on my agency — if they were 'slow-paying' on the check occasionally, I 'slow-did' the work. They would want to know when the next reports would come in, and I would say they'd get it when I got paid. It established a good pattern, where I got paid first and then did the work. If you work on the credit model, you will end up getting stuck with a bad debt at some point, which can be disastrous for an early-stage business.

When you're getting started, choosing the right business model has a big impact on your EHR. The option to work on retainer, pay-per-lead, or revenue share are all good options, or you can do one-time projects or recurring projects. You can have lots of products or just a handful (I generally advise people to steer clear of one-time products. It's a lot of work for a one-time result, and then you have to do it all over again, so it's exhausting. Focus on finding customers you can serve for a long time in a recurring way). Regardless, build long-term relationships with your clients and customers, and don't make short-sighted choices.

As soon as you can afford to, build a team around you to handle the things that are necessary but have a low EHR. Get good at leadership and finding the right people to help you build your business — you won't generate hundreds of thousands or millions of dollars in revenue every year if you're trying to do everything yourself.

Hiring is a hard skill set to develop and it's not intuitive, so the easiest way to get good people on board right early is to rely on referrals. Get referrals from business contacts who have had great experiences, and then once you've got a new team member, get referrals from them — people *they* know who would be good for your team. When I built my business out to 65 people, we never used a recruiter or a job board. I got a referral for the first person, and I hired the rest by word of mouth.

There are certain roles that the business owner shouldn't give up. Keep a really close hold on the financials — no one else should be able to generate checks or send money, because that's just asking for trouble. You'll also be responsible for the overall strategic vision of the company, what you want the company to be. It's up to you to create a mission that allows the rest of the people to support you in that vision. Eliminate everything you don't want to do, and spend most of your time focusing on your special area of genius, the thing that does make you really excited and happy, that you love doing and that fires you up.

13

MEET THE TEAM

As I mentioned earlier, the media buyer is only as good as their integration with the rest of the team.

The media buyer will only know what ads to run when they listen to insights from the social media manager and community manager that describe what the audience wants. The content marketer, channel marketer and developers provide the content and funnels the media buyer needs to drive and capture traffic in each campaign. The media buyer relies on the data scientist to help interpret all the information those campaigns generate, and to do predictive analysis on what will work in the future.

There are so many roles that need to be in play for businesses to be successful, and without these other roles, media buyers would be paralyzed. Like a family, every person brings a unique perspective to the mix, challenging each other and helping each other grow far beyond what they could do alone — which in turn, takes the business to a whole new level. This is good news too, because not everybody is cut out to be a media buyer.

In this chapter we're going to explore the other roles that

make up a digital marketing team. Some businesses will have huge teams with multiple people in each role, and others will have one person handling everything, but each role has a key part to play in the growth and success of every business operating in the digital space (and, I would argue, in traditional offline businesses too).

CONTENT MARKETER

Content marketers ensure that the content a business produces — blogs, videos, podcasts and many other formats — is shown to the right people, at the right time. The content marketer creates the assets that will move the audience through each of the eight stages of the customer value journey, so they have a critical role in attracting and retaining leads and customers.

To really understand content marketing, take a step back and think about how much information you get from the Internet. Think about how many Google searches happen every day, how many YouTube searches happen every day and so on. Now think about how many of those searches are made by people who want help with something that your business handles. The role of the content marketer is to anticipate those searches, to create material that will answer the question, and to make sure it's ranked effectively in the search results so that people find your content and are motivated to take another step towards working with your company.

Let me give you an example. A couple of years ago, my mom and step-dad came to visit me in San Diego during the Traffic & Conversion Summit where I was speaking. One day we were at lunch with Lindsay Marder, who was the editorial director for DigitalMarketer's content marketing team at the time. My parents understood that I bought

Facebook ads for a living, but they didn't quite get Lindsay's job.

We had been shopping that morning, because my step-dad needed some new jeans. He hadn't found anything he liked, so while we were sitting at lunch, he Googled "jeans for men with no butt." And a blog post came up that was titled precisely that — "Jeans for Men with No Butt." It was by Lucky Jeans, and it spoke directly to his problem. It addressed the frustration of not being able to find the right jeans for your frame, listed features to look out for that would make a pair of jeans more likely to suit you, and showed some options from their range that would be right for this particular audience segment. Later that afternoon, we walked past a Lucky Jeans store, and my step-dad went straight in and bought the pair of jeans they had recommended in the blog post.

As Lindsay pointed out that day, this is a perfect example of content marketing in action. It's about providing the information that customers want and need in order to make informed decisions about their purchasing. People want to understand their options and to feel informed in their interactions with businesses. Content marketing empowers the customer to make their best decisions, and allows the business to create and capitalize on buying intent. It's the interface between the expertise of the business and the customer's needs and desires.

A key part of successful content marketing is creating a strategy that actually serves the audience. A lot of people think of content marketing as just sitting down to write a blog post every week, and they don't give it much strategic thought beyond that. They're not thinking about whether the content they produce is meeting a real need in the audience, whether it will empower customers to make better buying decisions, or whether it creates or capitalizes on that buying intent. Effective content marketing is about answering the questions people want *your* company's answers to, and ensuring that they can find and engage with it easily.

CHANNEL MARKETER

This person is really focused on the back end of the funnel, the later stages of the customer journey. This role includes email marketing, chatbot marketing, SMS marketing and direct mail. It ensures that your team is utilizing all the communication channels available to you, after your audience has given you permission to follow up with them. Maybe the new subscriber gave you their email address, opted into Messenger marketing, or gave you their phone number or mailing address. The channel marketer then creates the next interactions that subscriber experiences with the business.

The channel marketer's job is to make sure that this next interaction (and every interaction thereafter) is positive and effective. They are responsible for the ongoing marketing your business sends to your audience, whether the audience has already purchased something from you and you would like them to purchase something else, or if they haven't yet made a purchase. The role includes making sure that subscribers are seeing good content, that you're continuing to build a relationship with them, and that they are receiving timely and tailored offers and messaging.

Part of this role is about creating promotional strategies each month, and working with the content manager to make sure that you're sending emails and messages to get more eyeballs on the content to build that relationship. This person looks at a lot of data to make sure they know how each channel is performing, and they know what types of emails, messages and texts to send out based on past performance. The channel marketer also works with the acquisition team to make sure that they know what type of leads are coming in, and what context those new leads are coming from. For example, if a new lead comes from a Facebook ad where there was a ton of discussion in the comment thread, the channel marketer should create an onboarding campaign that continues that conversation, and creates a very seamless transition for them into your marketing ecosystem.

Channel marketing is a very under-served position — you don't see it on many resumes, but it's such an important job, especially for an online business. It's a critical part of maximizing the lifetime value of your customers, and maximizing your per-transaction sales. The channel marketer can get a customer to come back to buy over and over again, far more than anyone else on the team. They are the mouthpiece of the business in communicating with the people who are already most likely to buy from you, and so it's a huge opportunity to bring significant revenue and profit into the business. It's a really important job.

This role seems to succeed best when the person has a good balance of analytical and creative capability, very similar to the media buyer. The relationship with customers has to feel very warm and human, with all the understanding and empathy people want, but that human element also has to be backed up with data — you have to be able to understand things like sender scores, list responsiveness and various other data points that will help you manage the audience effectively.

SOCIAL MEDIA MANAGER

This is the first role that many businesses hire for in digital marketing. I think that's because social media is a kind of 'gateway drug' into this whole space — a lot of business owners think they need to get online, start posting on Facebook, and then this whole digital thing will start to pay off. There's nothing wrong with starting that way, but a social media manager is *much* more than just someone who makes posts on a Facebook page.

A social media manager is most necessary for businesses that already have a big brand presence with a strong following and a lot of organic interest. This person is the voice and face of the company on public channels. Usually that's Facebook, Instagram, Twitter, YouTube, and it could also include Pinterest, LinkedIn and the various other platforms where your audience is hanging out. The social media manager should be present wherever your audience is, and they are responsible for engaging with that audience and attempting to drive organic traffic to your website or offer.

Their role is to ask the audience questions, share content, and even to post different sales or promotions that might be going on in the business. This person posts new information about the business, engages with the audience, builds the relationship and visibility your company has with them, and tries to grow that audience and reach new people too.

A big part of social media management is also listening to what is being said in and around your business and industry — using tools like Mention to see where your brand is being discussed online, to keep track of the wider conversations where you could get involved. This was something that I did at Buffalo Trace, the bourbon distillery I worked for in Kentucky before I got the internship at DigitalMarketer.

Every day, the first thing I would do was download an Excel sheet from some old software, and it would show me every place online that Buffalo Trace or any of its products had been mentioned in the last 24 hours. The technology has come a long way since then, but even that was really helpful in understanding how the brand was being perceived online.

It also helped me engage with the people publishing the material, since I could share that article, or I could comment and say thanks, or I could just engage with whatever conversation was already going on in response to the piece.

This role is not just about posting a bunch of stuff all the time and chatting away in the comments with people. It's a really important way of measuring the general feeling the audience has towards your brand, and understanding what they want from you. Listening to your audience can produce really valuable data that can impact the content marketing, the channel marketing, and even the offers and ads the brand focuses on.

Businesses have a direct line to their audience through social media, and so it can be a huge shortcut to finding out what's going on with them. The social media manager is usually the first to know if there's a customer service issue, often even before the customer service team, because they're right there on the front lines. That's why it's key that this person also works closely with the rest of the team, so that all this information can be passed on.

COMMUNITY MANAGER

Community managers also have a lot of interaction with the audience for your business, but where the social media manager is interacting with 'cold' prospects — mostly people who have never subscribed or bought anything from you — the community manager is interacting with people who *have* bought or subscribed. Because people now live so much of their life online, they are finding their tribes and congregating together online too, so community managers are hugely important in facilitating that around your brand. At DigitalMarketer, for example, we had DigitalMarketer Lab, which was a monthly membership, and part of that was that you got a private Facebook group where you could network and ask questions and interact with other members and the DigitalMarketer team.

Suzi Nelson, who was the community manager when I was there, really had a knack for this role. It's all about trying to get people to connect, and so Suzi was in this group all day, facilitating conversations. Part of the role was managing and moderating to make sure that the conversations were productive, but most of it was about talking to our customers, understanding what they all had in common, posting questions to drive conversation, and connecting them with one another so that they could all achieve their goals together.

Engagement metrics are the key success metrics here, and Suzi would report things like how many of the 10,000 or so members engaged in the group each week, what the response was to various discussions and so on. There's no direct response element there, but the people that were active in DigitalMarketer's group were also our best customers. They were the most loyal and the most invested of all the customer segments, and the most vocal about sharing DigitalMarketer with their networks. People in healthy online communities become brand ambassadors just by virtue of having such positive personal interactions with your company.

Some communities are hosted on Facebook, some businesses have them on their website, some of them are free, some of them are paid. But regardless of how they're structured, communities can be used at all steps of the funnel, and so community managers are becoming more and more important. Facebook is where most online communities live now, and those are going to continue to evolve. You definitely have to love people and want to bring them together to thrive in this role. You also have to be able to understand people and know how to facilitate a much more interactive relationship than the other roles in the digital marketing space. Having a community manager makes the business real to people — it takes it away from being purely transactional to being an actual relationship.

DATA AND ANALYTICS SPECIALIST

This is one of the most important roles, in any business, period. Never before have we been able to track and understand consumers like we can now. Every action someone takes online can be tracked, so you have to have someone that understands not only how to do the tracking (through tools like Google Tag Manager and Google Analytics), but also has a data-driven mind and wants to analyze the data to come up with ideas about how it can be used. That is the perfect package here.

This person makes sure that everything that *can* be tracked *is* tracked. But they're also there to interpret the data to inform the team about the opportunities the data is presenting. This person is obviously very analytical, and has to love numbers. But they also need to understand how digital marketing works, so that they can make sense of the numbers in relation to what the strategy should or shouldn't be, or why something is working or not.

John Grimshaw, who was the Data and Analytics Specialist at DigitalMarketer for several years, and now works with me on most of my projects, describes it like this:

 Looking at data is a really great way to back up your decision-making process with facts and information specific to your business. Typically this role is for a data analyst or a data scientist (who are analysts that can work with more code — analysts at heart with a developer shell).

Their job is to take all the raw information that people are generating on the company's platforms — the website, the customer relationship management tool, the email platform, the inventory management program and so on — then synthesize that information to point out opportunities and potential problems. For example, the data person might see that a product is running out, and can tell the email person not to promote it for a while, so they don't create a huge customer service problem. Or they might see that a page on the website is generating a lot of traffic, but there's no call to action for people to buy something — so they could suggest that adding a button would be an easy way to make more money there.

These are simple examples, but this role is about taking information from a bunch of disparate sources, and combining it with contextual information about the business. This should help the business owners and leadership make smart decisions about where to invest time, what new projects to work on, and where there are potential opportunities or pitfalls.

Being a data and analytics person isn't about just tracking the data — it's also about interpreting what it *means*. Maybe today there's a lot of extra traffic coming in from a holiday promotion, but are those extra people doing what you want them to? If not, why not?

What could change to get more people to take the action you're aiming for? This role is about going a step beyond just providing numbers and providing insight that relates to the business's goals and objectives. They're an interface between the business leadership and the business data.

———

There are dozens of roles in the digital marketing world. Every business that's growing will need their finances handled, design delivered and projects managed.

And if you're starting your own business, you might fulfill all these roles for a while — it's okay if you don't want to hire a whole team up front. There are as many different ways to do business as there are individuals starting businesses, so take what works for you and leave the rest.

We've explored media buying extensively, so now let's hear from the people that make the role of media buying possible. Each person profiled here generously gave me their time to share their insights on their role for this book, so I'm going to introduce each of them and then let them tell you about their expertise in their own words.

Don't worry if you don't see your existing skill set covered in the following profiles — it's simply beyond the scope of this book to highlight every single role in a digital business.

Each of these interviews is a few pages long, so you can either read through all of them in order if you're not sure which role might suit you, or dip into the profiles that interest you most right now. Either way, make sure you check out the final chapter once you're done — there are just a few more things you should know.

14

RUSS HENNEBERRY

OWNER AND PUBLISHER AT
WWW.MODERNPUBLISHER.COM

Russ was one of the first people I worked with in this industry at DigitalMarketer. He is a great friend and mentor to me, and he's been doing this for a long time. What's special about Russ is that he has taken so many paths to get to where he is today. He has gone back and forth between being an employee and running his own business a few times, and I love that he's allowed himself to be fluid and to take whichever path suits him and his family at different points in time. Russ is the first person that put this whole journey in perspective for me: he helped me understand that it doesn't really matter how you apply these skills to begin with: whether you're an employee or a business owner, you're building a valuable skill set that no one can take away from you.

Content is the building block of the digital world. Most of what we're doing online is consuming content, whether it's entertainment, education, or inspiration. The content marketer's role is to figure out how to produce content that can impact the metrics that are most important to the business they're working on.

A lot of the advice you will hear about content marketing is this kumbaya, wishy-washy, 'produce great content and everything will fall into place for you' nonsense. I'm here to tell you that's not true. Good content is not enough. Great content is not enough. *Amazing* content is not enough. If you're going to make a living at this, you've got to figure out how to make your content affect business metrics. You've got to be able to point to where the money is and to show the business owner where the results are coming from.

Having paid traffic on top of your content really accelerates that process and improves how those metrics are performing. This is why Molly might be the most important person I met in my entire career — when we worked out how content can be used in conjunction with paid traffic, it was game-changing. When we started to explore how it works when you have one person who's a master at producing the building blocks of content, and you have someone else who's a master of getting eyeballs on that stuff, it changed the whole way we thought about our marketing systems.

There are three stages that content marketing breaks down into — top of funnel (which is about creating awareness), middle of funnel (which is about education and lead acquisition) and bottom of funnel (which is about monetization and retention). I call these stages TOFU, MOFU and BOFU as a shorthand.

TOFU is where you're driving awareness. There are particular content types that work better here — blog posts, podcasts and videos. This is where you just focus on getting your business in front of a particular audience and making them realize that you exist and that you are interesting. You can advertise it and pay to get eyeballs on it, and then you get to MOFU. The key types of content here are lead magnets — checklists, ebooks, quizzes, webinars and so on that people to opt into. Then you get to BOFU, where you've got content that moves the lead towards the point of sale and the monetization stage. This kind of content includes demos and free trials, as well as comparison content (for example, showing how your product is different from a competitor's). After someone has bought from you, you have retention-based content to make sure that the people who are already paying you stick around (support material and success content).

Instead of starting with TOFU content, start at the other end with the BOFU content — these are what I call money pages. These are pages on your website where people can actually pull out their credit card and pay you. Start here, because it will generate the revenue that allows you to then take a step out and do more lead generation content, and then another step out to produce awareness content.

For example, recently I've gotten into mountain biking, and one night at home I was wondering what equipment I would need to get really good at this. Think about where I am at this stage — I'm already psychologically committed, my credit card is sitting right here on the table, I want to buy some stuff. I started Googling around and ended up on REI.-com, who sell outdoor equipment. They had a *very* exhaustive resource telling me everything I'm gonna need to be a mountain biker, and guess what? All those items had links to take you across to all the product pages.

That's a money page right there, and ultimately, any effective business owner is going to be most concerned with two metrics. They might track dozens or even hundreds of metrics across the board, but at the end of the day the only numbers that really matter are revenues and costs: how much money is coming in, and how much money is going out the door.

If you start to drill down into each one of those metrics, you start to think about how content affects acquisition — how much is it costing us to generate a lead? How much is it costing us to generate a closed sale? Cost per acquisition and cost per lead metrics are affected big time by the content that you produce.

I'll give you an example. You're sitting in a meeting as a content marketer and the big question in that meeting is how we are going to drive down the cost to acquire a customer. As the content marketer, your response should be to think about what content needs to be produced to educate and invite leads more effectively. What content can you hand over to new leads, or give to the people in sales that move those leads towards a sale, that will reduce the cost per acquisition?

When I worked at Salesforce, we called this 'sales-assisting content' and it's the absolutely critical part of content marketing that many people never think about. They think that writing a blog, making a podcast, or running a YouTube channel is content marketing — and don't get me wrong, I love all that stuff — but just making that content is not going to be enough to drive those two key metrics of money in and money out. I always tell people when you're gonna do content marketing, you want to start closest to the money.

Now, there are a few key skill sets and traits that are key for this kind of work. You need to be a good communicator, you need to have tremendous empathy, and you need to be a student.

It's also very helpful to be able to organize information in a clear and logical way, and to be able to get information out of your head and into the prospect's, in the way that the prospect needs to hear it.

The major thing you need to be figuring out when you get started is how to produce content (practicing the craft), and then how to produce *better* content. At the early stages, a junior content marketer should be learning about the audience, learning to empathize with the customer, really getting to know the market, and doing a lot of lever-pulling (like operating the content management systems, line editing for spelling and grammar, sentence structure, formatting, and so on), so that they're confident with the systems we use to produce and distribute content.

And then as you start to move up, your day-to-day starts to involve more planning. A mid-tier content marketer might be managing someone's blog or podcast. If you're solo, you'll be producing a lot of material as well as starting to think more strategically about the content. If you work in a team, you wouldn't necessarily produce the content at this level, but you're in charge of it — you're running the editorial calendar is, wrangling experts, editing the content for meaning, spending time on important elements of that content (perfecting the headline, the opening and closing material, the call to action and so on).

When you get to this stage, you have a better grasp on the ecosystem of the content and traffic sources you have available to you. You know the business's objectives, and the goals of the content that you're in charge of producing. You know your customer and audience very well, so you're able to make tweaks to content that someone less familiar with the audience produced, to make it more attractive to your audience.

Then at the very highest level of content marketing, you're setting strategy, and working with other leadership to set the direction of the business, using content as one of the vehicles to move the business forward. From there, you're able to see the bandwidth that the team has, what production capability you have, trying to make new partnerships with outside experts. You're basically managing an organization.

But no matter which level you're at, there's something a little bit magical about content marketing, because you can't put content marketing into a formula. I've watched people try to scale out content marketing into a mechanical process, but every attempt has been a waste of time, because there is something in the experience and insight that a great content marketer can bring to the piece of work. Their experience and skills always produce a unique perspective.

A lot of great content marketers have a really interesting background, and their experience means that they're very empathetic and communicative, but they also have that analytical, progress-focused outlook, and those two things together are very powerful. It's hard to train somebody for that if they haven't had the experience themselves, and that's what makes those people valuable.

A really powerful content marketer usually has a diverse range of experience and a lot of curiosity. If you're always wondering how things work, if you're always asking questions, if you're always reading or thinking or trying to absorb new information, looking at the world as a puzzle, then you're going to be good at this.

ARRI BAGAH

OWNER AND CHATBOT CHANNEL MARKETER AT WWW. ROASPOSITIVE.COM

When I met Arri, he was 21 years old and had built a chatbot agency called ROAS that was already working with multimillion-dollar companies like Guess, Poo-Pourri, and Beard Club. His family moved to the US from Togo in West Africa when he was a kid, and after brief stints studying pharmacy, gaming profession-ally on Twitch and serving in the Army reserve, he stumbled upon web development. He learned how to code, took some chances to build websites and e-commerce stores, learned some hard lessons and eventually found huge success with conversational marketing. Something that really stands out to me about Arri is his ability to say no. He has amazing boundaries, which is really important for a career on the Internet, because work is accessible to us everywhere. At such a young age, he's so wise and he's a huge inspiration to a lot of people already.

My agency is called ROAS Positive, and we grow revenue for e-commerce businesses by leveraging paid advertising and Facebook Messenger Marketing. I started in Messenger marketing when I got a job at an agency here in LA, managing the Messenger marketing service for all their e-commerce clients. I was the only one doing it, and at one point I was managing bots for over 15 clients. After I quit my job at the agency, I started my own company, leveraging my personal brand and that's how we were able to scale really fast and start working with some bigger clients.

Over the past decade or so, instant communication has become the standard way we communicate with friends, family, and coworkers. And because we got so used to instant messaging, we started expecting the brands and businesses that we communicate with to also communicate instantly. This meant that social media networks had to allow brands to leverage some sort of automation. Brands with even just 10,000 followers get so many messages that it becomes unmanageable to handle manually, even if you hire a lot of people. So all the social networks allowed businesses to set up bots on the platforms so that they could leverage instant communication for customer service and e-commerce.

So now, when people come on your site, you can have a Messenger opt-in pop-up, just like you have your email popup. You can even have an email pop up that has a Messenger opt-in connected to it, so that when people put in their email address, they also get subscribed to your Messenger list. The cool thing about Messenger is that it's so engaging, meaning that you're going to get super high open rates — most of our clients average between 80 and 90% open rates, and generally the click through rates are currently over 20%.

This is extremely powerful in the e-commerce space, and you can use bots at every stage of the funnel, but I've seen it work best at the bottom of the funnel. Once you've mapped out your customer journey, you can slot in messaging anywhere as a retargeting channel. We always try to fit it in where people drop off, usually once they've added some stuff to their cart.

Now, most people are on Facebook all day, so if they're dropped off your site, it's a good way to follow up with them. Your bot sends them a message, they open it, then click through to your site again. You can send them straight to the exact product they were looking at previously, which works really well — if somebody has added to cart, they've already expressed buying intent. So when you send them that message, they're more likely to convert. The average conversion rate for the cart recovery messages for a Messenger bot is between 15-20% (which is very high compared to the average conversion rate for an e-commerce site, which is 2-4%).

All this sounds really technical, but you don't need to be technical to be good at this. I didn't study marketing or do any formal training to get into this area. I actually dropped out of college twice! Most of this is not information that could really be taught in college, because it changes so much all the time. You just learn it by trying things out and doing a lot of research.

To build a great bot, there are three elements you need to get right. First, your bot should be as simple as possible. Second, you need to keep the audience engaged and deliver something they actually want. Third, you need to make sure that there are enough people actually seeing the bot to optimize it and make it pay off.

Most people think that their bots should have lots of complex features and capabilities. But this is a mistake. You should build the simplest bot possible to get the job done, and each bot should only have one job. Usually a basic build will give you 80% of the results you want or more. Build one bot to do one thing, and another bot to do another thing. When people try to make a single bot that does everything, they often don't even finish it because it's so complex, and even if you get it done, it's going to break with all the demands. Just keep things simple.

There are a lot of drag-and-drop bot building platforms right now. ManyChat is a pretty popular one, so anyone can get started creating simple bots. Some companies will need a developer to handle some technical integrations, but for most businesses, you don't need a lot of technical expertise to make a bot work for you.

Next, make your bot interesting! Most bots are so boring and they don't engage people. Imagine having a conversation with someone in real life — you have to keep them interested! As we all know, the attention span for most users online is super low, so you want to make sure that the copy is engaging and focused on what the customer actually wants. Make it feel fun and personal, because that's what people are used to experiencing on social media platforms. Don't be scared to use chatty language and emojis.

The last thing is to think like a marketer and maximize the number of people that are opting into your messenger marketing. You can have the greatest bot in the world, but it's useless if nobody sees it. You need to get traffic going to your site and to your channels so that you can actually optimize the conversation.

Remember that using bots is just another channel for serving your customers. The first thing you should do when you deploy this strategy is to let the consumer know they are interacting with a bot. Companies try to play it off like the bot is human, but inevitably the customer works out that this isn't the case, which breaks their trust, and then they never come back. So let people know it's a bot, and give them the option to continue with the bot, or to wait longer for a response from an actual person.

When you set up bots, it's super important to have humans to check in to make sure everything is going okay. If the bot fails, you want to notify a person to make sure that they're able to rescue any bad experience a customer might be having. You also need to make sure there's a team on-hand for the customers who still want to talk to a person rather than interacting with a bot.

Most platforms will allow you to set up notifications to notify somebody on your team automatically when something happens. I think the best plan is to use a combination of automation and human power. Automation helps you become more efficient and it gets rid of all the repetitive tasks that people have to do. When we take a look at the inbox of an e-commerce brand, I think 75% to 90% of the inbox can be automated, but the remaining 10 to 25% needs still needs a human.

Drift, a conversational marketing platform, published a in 2018 showing that 60% of people want to use a bot for instant responses and to be able to get 24/7 support. It's actually a much better customer service option than having a person do it in a lot of cases, and a lot of people still get excited about interacting with a bot. They like to try to test it out, and try to break it (which is another reason your bot should only do one thing!).

But there's still that 40% that want to interact with a real person, and we have to respect that. Some marketers think because you can use automation now, then you have to basically get rid of humans. You do not. Humans are still cool. We're still necessary. AI and machine learning are improving every day, but they're still not at the same level as humans for problem-solving and communicating effectively.

People used to call me crazy for thinking that messaging

is gonna be the future, but the best marketers in the future are going to be focused on how you can leverage messaging as a marketing channel, and how you can send the right message to the right customer at the right time.

Using bots is a completely different way to think about connecting with your audience for many marketers, but for people who have grown up using messaging apps, it's very native and easy, because it's what we're already doing. It's a great opportunity if you're completely comfortable with social media and understand how to communicate naturally with people on these platforms.

JOHN GRIMSHAW

DATA AND ANALYTICS AT WWW.SMARTMARKETER.COM
(TRAIN MY TRAFFIC PERSON & TEAM TRAFFIC)

John is one of the closest people to me in this industry and I've had the great fortune of watching him grow so much over the last several years. I hired John in 2014 as a marketing associate, and while he's a great generalist who really understands every aspect of marketing, he understood that he needed to specialize to really make his mark. He first worked for a software company, then he worked at DigitalMarketer, and now he's out on his own working with clients. He's partnered with Ezra and I at Smart Marketer on Train My Traffic Person and Team Traffic. He has this data-driven, analytical brain that he uses to make great decisions, and he has a broad generalist understanding that allows him to be so powerful. He's such an empathetic person, which really allows him to understand how other people are feeling, which is the most important aspect of marketing. This industry and career can bring so many wonderful people into your life, and like Russ, John is one of the greatest gifts I've gotten out of this whole journey.

In business, you're always trying to make decisions that help you earn more money, generate more customers, and keep people coming back. None of that's new, but it's not instinctive either. Trying to figure out the right decisions requires some sort of barometer or tool — a lot of people rely on their gut, but it doesn't really work, especially as your business gets bigger.

That's why there's a place in most companies for a data analyst or a data scientist (who can work with more code).

Their job is to take all of the raw information that people are generating on the company's website, the customer relationship management tool, the email platform, the inventory management program, all the different tools used in the business, and then synthesize that information to make decisions. They can point out when a product is running out, and highlight to the leadership that a sales email scheduled for tomorrow might cause a huge customer service problem. Or they might see that a page on the website is generating a lot of traffic, but there's no call to action for people to buy something, and can suggest that an easy way to make more money would be to have a button there where people can buy a product.

These are simple examples, but it's about looking at information from a bunch of disparate sources, and combining it with contextual information about the business. This helps the business owners and leadership to make smart decisions about where to invest time, new projects to work on, and where there are potential opportunities or pitfalls with the big picture solution that they're working on.

It's about interpreting what the data means, going a step beyond providing numbers to providing insight that relates to the business's goals and objectives. The data analyst is the interface between the business leadership and the business data.

There are not a lot of KPIs for data analysts in a digital marketing team, so in trying to evaluate my own performance, I look at how many ideas I am generating, and then how well those ideas perform for the company when implemented.

I keep a list of ideas that we could experiment with to improve the business's performance. (For example: run a promotion on Black Friday; improve this piece of the site where people are dropping out of the purchasing process; fix this supply chain issue that we've got because that's slowing down the experience and making customers unhappy.) Then whenever we actually implement one of those, I keep track of how much it impacts the business's performance, and that's how I judge my success or failure.

Any time we test something, the key for me is to go back and objectively evaluate whether it translated into growth for the company, whether it was a good investment of time. I'm not knocking points off my performance if it didn't work, because that's still valuable information. I would only knock points off if an experiment didn't work and then it was allowed to continue running for an unnecessary period of time.

In any business setting, you have to try to keep your emotions out of the decision-making, which of course can be very difficult. The analyst is a crucial check-and-balance role, because if you're in a situation where people are punished when experiments don't work, you can end up with people massaging the performance data so that everything looks amazing. The analyst is really set apart from all that, because their entire role is to correctly aggregate and interpret the numbers. They keep the team honest, and they protect the team if someone is looking for a scapegoat for something that didn't work. The data really doesn't lie.

This role relies on independent thinking, and being proactive in looking for opportunities where you can apply the data without necessarily being told where to focus by the leadership.

It also requires a surprising amount of creative thinking. You're not going to grow the company if you can't think outside the box a little bit. Some data people think of their role as an analyst as just to report the numbers — say, how many visitors are coming to a particular page, what the conversion rates are and so on, but that's a very incomplete picture. When someone can take that information and turn it into something actionable, that's when this role starts to become really powerful.

You have to be able to imagine opportunities and possibilities from the information you're collecting. This requires an ability to synthesize the raw numbers and interpret their collective meaning, along with being able to keep an open mind about what to do with that information.

Being very detail-oriented is extremely important, because mistakes made with figures can be multiplied by a factor of ten or more when you're helping the leadership to drive the direction of the business. If you think a particular investment should generate a significant ROI for the business, but your calculations are off, the company might spend a massive amount of money and never see a return, which can obviously have really serious ramifications.

You need to be able to future-cast, too — to be able to project how today's events will impact what happens twelve months from now. That's using statistics and being able to build out predictive models to demonstrate what a particular course of action will mean for the company along a particular timeline.

Reporting is a huge part of the data and analytics role, because your job is to communicate to people what worked, what didn't work, and what the takeaway action items need to be from that. You need to be able to make sure that people internalize the big idea and big lesson, and don't get stuck on whether a particular campaign won or lost. Instead, you need to drive people's focus to what the data *means*, extrapolating it to continue building the future of the company. You must be a clear communicator and be able to translate all the numbers and data into words that everyone on your team really understands.

In terms of actual qualifications, a knowledge of statistics is probably the most helpful of all the different mathematics, because you need to understand probability and percentages. Thinking in terms of percentages is really important because it allows you to compare disparate values. If you are comparing days when you have 1000 visits on the site and 10 sales, with days when you have 5000 visitors and 60 sales, it's not immediately obvious which is doing better. Converting stuff into percentages allows you to say, this one had a 1% conversion rate, and this one had a 1.2% conversion rate. The 5000 visitors is better, but not just because it was more people — the overall performance compares favorably.

Thinking in terms of ratios allows you to compare different businesses, and to compare different products and channels as well. When you're doing this modeling, or when you're helping people decide what project to invest time and energy in, you can use statistics to indicate the type of lift the business could expect from a particular plan. You need to be able to predict the statistical significance of a change, to be able to model it out. You don't really need calculus or geometry or anything like that — statistics and a little algebra will get you there. Again, you need to be detail-oriented, analytical, and you need to be able to at least use numbers to make decisions, but you don't need a degree in mathematics to do this.

A typical day in this role involves a lot of communication, so this is another thing you need to be quite competent with. I usually spend the morning reviewing the business's key metrics (these will depend on your specific business, but just do a health check on whatever the business's key metrics are to make sure that those look healthy). If those have an issue, then you need to change your day to focus on solving that problem.

After that, the next couple of hours are spent working with different teams or people at the company. Checking in regularly allows you to create the context that informs the meaning of the data. You need to understand the situations or problems that other teams are facing. For example, if the customer service platform broke down and consequently, there's a much higher volume of unhappy customers, that could explain why you suddenly have more bad reviews or returns than normal. Keeping abreast of whatever's going on in their specific world lets you make smarter decisions when you're looking at the raw data.

So the morning is usually that human interaction piece, and then in the afternoon, it would be more focused on reporting. This is when you look at the data related to whatever problem or idea you're focusing on at the time. If you're looking for ideas for growth, you might just freewheel it and look around at data from the website, or data from the inventory. Then once you've got an idea of what you want to focus on, you drill in and try to understand what's going on. Then once you've started to pull some data together, you actually start writing reports up. For example, you might see that you're spending all of your Facebook ad budget on a particular sales funnel, so you could come up with two ways to optimize it, and also suggest taking 10% of the budget and putting it into this new funnel, since the older funnel is showing signs of fatigue.

That analysis and reporting piece is the biggest chunk of the role. About 10% of this time is identifying what I specifically want to dig into that day, 50% doing the actual research, and then the last 40% is writing my notes and analysis.

When picking what to focus on for a day, I use what I call the analytical decision making process, which is essentially just the scientific method. It's identifying a problem or an opportunity — sales are way up, sales are way down, leads are way up, leads are way down, it could be almost anything — and trying to identify the cause of this change. Maybe it's a good change, maybe it's a bad change, but either way, you run through this process of asking yourself questions and forming hypotheses about why that's the case.

You go through and look at supporting metrics, or what I call drill-down metrics, to validate or disprove that hypothesis. By the end of it, you can see that sales were way up, and a small part of the reason is that it's summer-time and we sell bathing suits. But a large part was that this influencer on Instagram posted a picture wearing our bathing suit. Another little bit of it is that we had a lot of customers refund in the last 30 days, and they all came back and bought a different suit. You run through maybe 20 different hypotheses, but you end up with just three that you can prove with data. Then you would take that into the next morning's meetings, and keep a conversation going about what you're finding and what the other teams are finding.

This role is very cool, when you work at the right place, because you will be working with all different kinds of teams, you'll have very direct connections with the leadership. I find this role to be way more fun when you're working at a company that's interested and invested in using data, and when you're working at a small to medium business.

LAURA PALLADINO

SOCIAL MEDIA STRATEGIST AT
WWW.SMARTMARKETER.COM

I really respect Laura's growth in this game. She started out working at Cracker Barrel, and worked her way up at Smart Marketer and Boom!, and the reason she's done so well is that she's always trying to figure out what's working. Whenever I see Laura, she's chatting about experiments she's trying on social and in email — she's always pushing something forward. Laura has become the go-to person for me when I'm trying to work out how something is working on social, and I love the positive energy she brings to everything. She cares about other people deeply (which is clearly a theme among all these people) and is really making the most of her opportunities, growing into speaking and teaching and she's a great example of how this industry can completely change your life.

A few years ago, Ezra Firestone moved to the town where I live. He happened to walk into the Brazilian Jiu-Jitsu gym I own with my husband, and we became pretty close friends. I was working at Cracker Barrel as a waitress to bring in some more money, and one day Ezra asked if I was happy there. It was making me money but it wasn't particularly enjoyable. Ezra's team at Boom! were experiencing an influx and needed help with customer support, so he invited me to transition over to working with them.

When I first started, I was answering phone calls, refunding people, dealing with pretty standard customer service stuff. About a year in, Ezra came to me and asked if I wanted to move to social media. We weren't doing much on the organic side of social media yet — we were running ads but weren't just producing content and engaging with people — so I jumped in the deep end. I went to conferences, read a bunch of books, followed lots of blogs, and started trying to figure things out to really make our social channels work, and eventually I ended up leading a whole team.

I love this role, because I can really work from anywhere as long as my laptop is with me. I'm not a 'digital nomad,' I haven't started traveling all the time, but I have so much more flexibility. It's still work, obviously, but if I'm just having one of those days, I can shut my laptop and go take a walk. I don't have to ask my manager if it's okay that I go outside for a few minutes. I also get to do my work at my own pace, and my work is valued.

In my previous jobs you were really only valued as just a worker, a cog in a machine, whereas in this type of environment, we all depend on each other to make the whole system work. I think that gives us all a much bigger sense of purpose, and because we're helping out other businesses, there's a bigger picture to this type of work than there ever was before. I have more independence and autonomy, and a sense of value and purpose from the work, and I'm learning all the time.

Social media changes drastically every day. Being the lead social media strategist is about keeping up with all that change, figuring out the best way to engage our community, and revamping our strategies as needed for our social, email and content strategy. There's no such thing as a normal day in this job — it's all over the place because things change so often.

I do spend a lot of time diving into our analytics to understand what's working and what new strategies we can implement in the coming months. If we have a sale going on, there's a lot of promotional work that happens on social, but other regular tasks include managing email promotions, organizing all of our content, and syndicating it to the various platforms it will be shared on. For example, when we have one piece of content, let's say it's a video, we will split it up into shorter segments and those go to Facebook, Instagram posts and stories, it goes to email, the blog, and so my job on a day-to-day basis is organizing the flow of all of that and looking for ways we can improve that each time.

To do well in this role, you have to be able to decipher the analytics, and to have a lot of attention to detail. Little things are going to change your strategy in a big way, so you really have to pay attention to all the changes on each platform, and study the analytics to see what those changes mean for your audience. I also create a lot of SOPs, and am focused on systematizing all of our processes for social, email and content distribution, so that anyone on our team can handle any piece.

You also have to be comfortable with other people, there is an element of extroversion to this. You have to be able to talk with your team and communicate well, and you have to be able to shut off everything and go into a more introverted mode too, to learn and absorb all the new information coming in all the time. You can't constantly be in 'busy mode', because you have to pause long enough to really think and strategize.

A huge part of this role is about asking questions. Anyone can do this if you have the right mindset. Wanting to learn, and being confident enough to ask questions is the most important thing. I tell my team all the time not to apologize for asking questions, because none of it's intuitive. You can't go to college right now and learn any of this. It's all coming at you on a day-to-day basis and the algorithms and rules and strategies are changing all of the time, so really the most important thing is curiosity, confidence in asking questions, and a willingness to learn and adapt.

The KPIs we track are mostly around social proof — figuring out what the engagement rate for each campaign is like. We look at the total number of followers versus how many people are engaging with posts (if you have a million followers but you're only getting a few people engaging there needs to be a content strategy change, for example). The total follower growth on all the platforms is something to track quarterly and annually. We also track content trends, so for example, if your brand only ever posts videos and you've never tried something else, we would definitely try turning those videos into articles, quote posts and so on to see what the effect on engagement is.

There are so many different ways to start improving your social channels that you can feel kind of paralyzed trying to work out which is going to be the best way. But my biggest piece of advice is just to test what you think is going to work. Think about what makes sense to you, and pick one thing to test. Make a hypothesis about what's going to happen, develop a clear reason you're testing this idea, and if it doesn't work, study the analytics to figure out why. Then test something else, and just repeat that over and over until you feel confident in your understanding of each area. Find one piece, really study that, and let your understanding build up gradually, as opposed to trying to learn everything all at once. And finally, remember that everyone has been there. Everyone was once at the beginning, and had no idea what was going on. When you start asking questions, researching and testing, and learning from other people, you start to develop the skills and confidence you need to be really effective.

18

SUZI NELSON

Community Manager

Suzi was working at a local dance studio when I hired her to join the DigitalMarketer team back in 2014. She dove right in, and she's a great example of someone who is willing to try new things. Even if she's scared, she pushes through. There was no clear guidebook for online community management, there was no formal education for it, and Suzi has become one of the best community managers in the world. She really cares about the communities she manages, and she really cares about bringing people together online. She understands that social media can be really polarizing, and she has made it her mission to use these platforms to bring people together. I very much admire her for that and for taking the leap to move to California to work in community management for one of the biggest tech companies ever created.

Community management is about bridging the gap between the company, their content and product, and the customers.

The role is about adding humanity back into marketing. It's about talking with people, and having real authentic relationships, one-on-one and one-to-many. It's community marketing.

While people throw the word 'community' around a lot as a buzzword, it actually has a really clear definition: a group of people who are passionate about something they have in common. They have a bond around a particular interest, and if your brand is associated with that bond, you have a community that you can tap in to.

The key focus is to foster communication between your community members. It's removing the broadcasting element of marketing, and turning it into an actual conversation. Instead of just giving your audience a big chunk of information and getting nothing back, you're connecting members with each other, you're inspiring greater discussions among people, you're making people feel like they are a part of something unique and special.

Community management is grounded in behavioral psychology. A lot of companies hire community managers who are inexperienced, because they assume it's an easy role. But those same companies get into trouble, because community management is a lot harder than it looks.

The science that underpins this role comes from research done over the last few decades to find out what makes healthy communities in the offline world. It turns out that when we gather online, we behave similarly to how we behave in offline communities, like we do in churches, and with friends. It all follows the same format.

One of the models that I'm a big fan of is the relationship model by George Levinger. Levinger studies how relationships form (whether that's a romantic relationship, a platonic relationship, or an acquaintance). He mapped out a linear sequence that happens whenever we meet someone, that allows us to go from being acquaintances, to being friendly, to being very close. When you understand that framework, you can go in and create community content that moves people along that journey in online groups too.

Another cornerstone theory that I use every single day is called Sense of Community. The sense of community theory is that when people gather together, there are four elements that make them feel like they are a part of something cool and bigger than themselves: membership, influence, integration or fulfillment of needs, and shared emotional connections. If you understand those four elements, you can create content that influences how people feel about being a part of this community. This is different to the actual function of the community — which is to improve the long-term health of the business.

A lot of businesses get really caught up in just broadcasting to their community instead of really *engaging* with them. I get how tempting that is — you have a group of interested people right there in one spot, but your community space is not for selling. It's for nurturing that sense of community in your leads and customers so that when they receive a piece of marketing separately, through an email or an ad for example, they actually *want* to take action and stay connected to this awesome brand.

Marketing is all about putting the right message in front of the right people at the right time. Community is part of that, building that sense of community should be your North Star whenever you're creating to generate that engagement. Every piece of content needs to move people through that relational model a little bit further, taking them from being an acquaintance, to being a friend, to being part of an inner circle that actually includes everyone in the group.

To do this, you need to get some self-disclosure from each new member — getting them to share something about themselves that generates discussion, with questions like, "what's your biggest challenge with [your niche here] right now?" This gives people a chance to share something meaningful, and gets other members to engage and share themselves. But getting someone to post once is not enough, and so the following few days are very intentional in continuing those conversations so that members feel like they're getting the information they want and that their social needs are being met by peers they can trust in this group.

That's why community managers need to be really clear about which part of the audience is in the community. Prospects need more educational content and more ways to connect with each other, while existing customers need more content that increases the value of their experience and gives them more reasons to continue engaging with the business. Know who your community is serving, and make sure that it's not serving everybody at once, because then you'll just miss the mark.

Reporting on the ROI value of community really depends on where your community fits into the customer journey. If you're nurturing leads for example, your reporting would focus on lead generation, brand awareness, offer awareness. You should see things like direct traffic to your website go up. In the middle of the funnel, you're looking for things like customer retention, increased frequency and recency of sales, increased testimonials and word of mouth. At the bottom of the funnel, you start seeing things like increased affiliate sales, increased lifetime value, reduced churn and so on.

It's very easy to *correlate* ROI with community, but it is quite difficult to *attribute*. I usually warn brands that you'll be able to see trends, but because cross-platform attribution is so difficult, and data protection is getting more and more strict, you're probably not going to get all the data on actual performance that you would like.

Because this is a newer role in the industry, a lot of community managers find themselves having to justify the community to their bosses. It's important to develop the skill of advocating for your community internally, which means being able to talk about it in terms of reducing cost, or increasing revenue, and learning how to use the language of business leadership to communicate the value of what you're doing. A lot of communities struggle to really get traction because their community managers are inexperienced and are not involved in setting the strategic intent for the community.

In addition to being willing and able to advocate for your community, you need to bring a hunger to learn. This is such a dynamic industry and it will really set you apart if you can apply yourself to learning these processes. Being able to articulate what connects human beings is mind-blowing to a lot of clients — while the need for connection is hardwired into us, most people can't communicate why it's so important. You need the ability to take that transactional relationship and make it emotional, because emotional connections are much stronger and last much longer than the connection someone gets from just buying something from you.

And even though communities vary quite a bit, most community managers will spend most of their time building those connections. The common threads will be welcoming new members, and making sure the right members are coming in. You're making sure that people understand the rules, and you're looking out for opportunities to build sense of community in the discussions taking place. You should be looking out for questions that are being asked repeatedly, then going off to create a piece of content to proactively answer it.

You'll also do a lot of moderating, which means that if somebody's being a jackass, you have to deal with it diplomatically and constructively — so that the community actually improves from the incident. You'll also be gathering feedback about what has happened recently in the community, and reporting this to other teams you're working with. You're basically talking to people all day long, on both sides of the relationship, to make sure that the conversations that are happening are valuable and productive. Most of the day goes to proactive facilitation, reactive moderation, and strategic implementation.

Something that really helped me get a grip on all this was to start researching how the individual brain works. If you understand the individual, you can understand the group. So I started reading books about behavior, how to form habits, how to influence behavior in other people, and about marketing generally. Marketing is all about getting people to take action, and that's what community is all about. You're getting them to respond and engage. You're not just following your community wherever it goes — you're leading this community.

19

COLLEEN TAYLOR

PROJECT MANAGEMENT AND CHIEF OPERATING OFFICER AT
WWW.SMARTMARKETER.COM

Colleen was my first manager at DigitalMarketer — my first boss — and thank God that she was. She really brought that feminine, caring energy to a very male-dominated environment, and I wouldn't still be doing this stuff without her. When I was hired full-time after interning at DigitalMarketer, I was trying to find my place, working like crazy, and Colleen checked me that there's more to life than work, but most importantly, she rallied for me. Colleen saw who I could be before anybody else, and she really fostered that. When she left the company, we maintained our friendship, and now it's a total joy to get to work with her again. Colleen really exemplifies what it means to make the most of this career path. Her superpower is her ability to care for people and I appreciate her more than I can say.

I think relationship building is the single most important

part of how digital marketing will unfold into the future. Ultimately, it always comes back to human connection. There are a lot of people who feel very isolated by how much digital interaction is taking over, and they miss that human interaction. And digital will never be able to replace the human connection, no matter how efficient it becomes. This is one reason that looking for fulfillment in your work is so important.

One of my mentors put it like this to me many years ago: "When you start to feel doubt or dissatisfaction about the impact of your work, trust your gut and answer one simple question: is this the hill you want to die on? And if the answer is no, if this is not the thing you are prepared to give everything to, start making your exit plan so you can get to work on the hill you would die on."

My formal education was in fine arts and graphic design in New York. After realizing that I couldn't afford to live in the city on an artist's income, I decided to move to California after I graduated. I arrived in San Diego with $75 and a credit card, and figured I would work it out. This was in 1997, and I ended up working with a web start-up providing customer service to all these people who were learning to use the Internet for the first time.

Like most internet start-ups at the time, they eventually ran out of money, but during the five or six months I was there, the knowledge I was exposed to just blew my mind.

Their website was the first I'd ever seen, and the guy who owned the company explained it all to me. He showed me all the standard pages, and it all made sense to me, but the whole thing just looked like crap. The graphic design was terrible and so everything I had learned in my degrees came rushing back to me. I told him that if he fixed the design, people would feel better about using the website and would feel more confident buying his services, so he said he would show me how to start working with the design elements. He showed me that when you right-click on a page, you can select 'view source' from the pop-up that appears, and it will display all the code that determines how that page looks. He explained that HTML meant HyperText Mark-up Language, and I was hooked.

I knew that if it was a language, I could learn it, it seemed really mathematical and cool, so from that moment I started going in to work early to view the source code of all the pages I could access. I started making suggestions and changes to make it look nicer (the main search engine at this time was Metacrawler, so SEO really hadn't become a consideration yet).

I really wanted to learn how to create these pages, so I would go to the library — the actual brick and mortar library — and check out as many mark-up language books as I could find. I didn't have a computer at home, so I would take a pencil and notebook and copy out code from these library books, longhand. Then after work the next day I would type all the code in, then view the page so I could actually see what I'd just made.

Step by step, I learned how to build pages, change layouts and code in that old-school HTML, and it was the start of a deep love of digital. Over the next few years I built a whole business around creating websites for local businesses, and I did a lot of work with the CFO of that very first web start-up. One day in late 2004 he called me up with a new opportunity, with a guy named Eben Pagan.

Eben had started with a free newsletter. Then he wrote a book, and people were willing to pay for it because he had led with value first. The book absolutely blew up online. He had thousands of customers and he had a website, but he needed all kinds of sales pages and funnels to be built, and no one on his team knew HTML. He wanted to build a follow-up course to the book, and so this is where we started to really see the beginning of online marketing. He was split-testing all kinds of things, making sure things were attributed correctly, so I was learning new things about digital marketing, information products and funnels every single day I worked for him.

Eben was one of the very first people to develop an ecosystem of products online and this is where it really all came full circle for me — this was how people would make money online. When I first got started all the way back in 1997, I never thought the Internet would last, because I couldn't see how people would sustainably make a living. But now I saw the money, and it was because I saw the relationship component of marketing in action.

Eben was so focused on building the relationship first, so we weren't in a rush with people. We took our time to nurture them through all the products, and we did it carefully so that each time they were offered something it was at the right time and in the logical order according to what they had already consumed from us. It was very tailored. I worked for Eben for nearly eight years, then I went to DigitalMarketer, which is where I met Molly.

I also met Ezra while working at DigitalMarketer, where I was the project manager for a product we were launching for him there. After I left, Ezra eventually reached out looking for a project manager. I was running my own agency by then, so I agreed to consult with him as a client until they found the right person to join the team full-time. I was committed to doing my own thing at that stage, but over the next few months his team really impressed me.

Instead of leading with fear, pressure and stress, Ezra leads by celebrating what's going right, making people feel good about themselves, and creating an environment where people are prioritized over ticking off tasks. He articulated everything I had ever felt about working in teams, and so in the end I let all my clients go and went to work with him full-time, because I believe in his mission, both for the business and out in the world, and it's very clear to me that this is the kind of hill I would be willing to die on.

It's always about the team and the people for me, because when you're in operations or working as a project manager, you're not really managing projects at all — you're managing people. You're managing people's feelings and motivations and handling all the different personality types.

Some corporate teams want to see everything perfectly laid out in their project management software with every box ticked, all done exactly on time and they want to analyse every detail afterwards. There's nothing wrong with any of that, but when doing everything perfectly becomes the motivating factor for getting a project done, not taking into account the humans that are delivering the project, that's when things go wrong.

Humans always have life happening to them, and you need to factor that into how you plan and manage your projects. People get sick and have kids and need vacations and have car crashes and dependent parents and so many other things. Project managers always have to remember that people are the ones doing the tasks, and without people to do them, the tasks don't get done. When you take care of the people, you take care of the tasks.

Of course, you have to hire the right people, and the thing we're looking for most often in employees is that they want to improve things for other people. They genuinely want to improve other people's lives, in whatever way that is for their particular set of abilities. We look for people who are not just looking to get paid or to get a cool reference on their resume — we're looking for people who want to be part of something meaningful and who want to have a real impact on the lives of the people we're serving.

Hiring people like this makes it a joy to build strong relationships with your team, and it's much easier to create an environment where your team can tell you anything, where nothing that is happening to them is off-limits. If your people know they can tell you everything that's happening to them and that you will be in their corner, they'll do great work for you. It's when they don't feel they can tell you things that you start to have problems.

It's about transparency. I want my people to tell me everything. I always tell people, "don't flake, don't just not show up, just tell me, and we'll work it out together. If the timeline can be moved, it will be moved, for you." People on our team are not just cogs in a wheel, and they understand that, unlike in many corporate situations, they're not going to get in trouble if they need to change a timeline. Everybody has an important role in getting our projects done, so if you need something — more time, support, or resources — I want to hear about it and help.

Everybody matters in this equation. When you have empathy and rapport, everything else falls into place. When your people trust, yours will always be a hill they're willing to fight on.

20

AN INVITATION

There has been a huge amount for you to absorb in this book, and I hope you'll come back to it whenever you need some new ideas, some clarification, or when you just need a boost. A lot of the information is technical, but I think the most important parts are about balance, and about creating the mindset that is going to allow you to thrive in this new digital economy. I'd like to wrap up here by sharing something Ryan Deiss said during our interview for this book. I don't share this to make myself look good, but to highlight a few characteristics that matter more than anything else if you're going to create a life you really love: being fearless, humble, and coachable.

 When Molly started as an intern at DigitalMarketer, we needed someone on Facebook ads, and when I asked the team who was willing to try, Molly put up her hand. She went out on a limb and tried something new that she could have easily failed at. She was willing to take direction, and she put in a lot of work to get really good at what she was doing.

That's why Molly ascended so quickly through DigitalMarketer. Yes, the timing was right for her, but she rose so quickly because she was teachable, she was fearless and she invested tremendously in her own growth.

Whether it was running Facebook ads for the first time, or getting on stage in front of thousands of people, it didn't matter whether she was ready or not, because she's fearless. That's the core of being a good marketer. You have to be somewhat fearless, which means being willing to make mistakes and feel foolish sometimes. It's going to be hard because you will lose money — either your own, if it's your company, or the company's money. Some people will never be okay with that, but you have to be willing to keep trying until you find a way forward. Molly has been doing that since day one.

And because she approached her leadership with both competence and humility, people actually followed her. You know you're a leader when you turn around and there are people behind you, and Molly is very much that person.

At the start of this book I told you there was one more life-changing decision I had to tell you about. Well, by the end of 2017, I was ready to get out of Austin. I was burned out, exhausted by city life and desperately needing to reconnect with myself. So in 2018 I moved out to Telluride,

Colorado — a beautiful little town nestled at the base of a huge mountain range, and home to a grand total of 2500 people. It was incredibly peaceful. I would wake up in the mornings to see herds of deers wandering through my yard, or the occasional bear climbing over the fence. The summer was warm and perfect for hiking, and the winter was breathtaking as snow piled up quietly around my house.

Slowly, being in the mountains healed all the stress and burn-out that had accumulated over the past decade, and I started to feel more in touch with what I wanted to do with this next stage of my life. As I started feeling restored, it was time to start moving again. I was 29 years old, and wanted to go someplace that would energize me for this next step of building and scaling this business with Ezra, John and the Smart Marketer team. My lease expired at the end of the spring in 2019, and it was time for something new.

I decided to go to Amsterdam for the summer before deciding where to settle next. It's a beautiful city, it has that vibrant city energy without being too intense, there are lots of digital marketers and it's easy to get to from New York where Ezra and the team are if I needed to visit. About six weeks in, I met an American woman who lived there. She had opened up a business under the Dutch-American Friendship Treaty, and so had received a visa to become a resident… and that sealed it. I stayed.

Amsterdam is an amazing place to live. It's a great stop on people's European trips, so friends visit often, and because it's a few hours ahead of the US, I have each morning to myself to do whatever I need to make sure my life is in balance. Europeans have a view on life that I really appreciate — they prioritize work-life balance and they spend more time with friends, eating together and staying connected with their families.

This little container I've built for myself in Amsterdam feels very safe and exciting for me, and is really helping to propel me to the next step of my career. But if you had told me a few years ago that I would be living in Europe, working from an office that overlooks a leafy canal, taking a few calls in the afternoon and then spending each night with friends or wandering the old alleyways with my dog... I would have thought it was impossible.

But it's all possible, and it's possible for you too.

Not long before arriving in Amsterdam for that summer, I joined forces with Ezra Firestone to collaborate with his awesome team at Smart Marketer. We launched a program called Train My Traffic Person, which was a major success, and so Ezra and I decided to take it to the next level by adding some more products to the mix, and brought John Grimshaw on board to help us make that happen. I realized that while I enjoyed working with clients from time to time, I can make the biggest impact on this industry by teaching. I'm able to help a hundred people at a time instead of a handful of people individually. Teaching is so fulfilling, and it makes my life a lot easier — I'm on less calls, I'm able to hire people to help grow the business, and it's a much more scalable business model for me and my lifestyle than serving individual clients or building an agency would have been.

After Train My Traffic Person, we also added Team Traffic, which is a monthly membership for ongoing education. We've also been able to launch Smart Traffic Live, which is an annual online event all about paid traffic, where we bring a bunch of lovely people together (like many of the people you met here in this book) to teach about paid traffic. We were able to do over seven figures in revenue in the first year, which is exciting, but I'm even happier at the freedom this new model has given me.

This moment in history, where digital is changing everything, can change everything for you too, and I invite you to take the next step: acquire the knowledge, build the skill set, and actually apply it all. This is *your* life, and this is your moment to let that *click* happen, so that you can live anywhere, work on your own terms and become the happiest version of yourself you can possibly be.

READY FOR THE NEXT STEP?

You've learned a lot in this book, and the most important thing now is to start putting it into action.

That's why I've put together a big ol' resource page for you to help you take the next steps towards building a life and career you truly love.

Go to www.mollypittman.com/clickhappy today to get your downloads, courses, and bonus content.

You'll also find links there to the Train My Traffic Person course and the Team Traffic membership, along with video trainings, podcasts, new posts and more.

See you in digital!

Molly.

ACKNOWLEDGMENTS

A huge, huge thank you to everybody who helped make this book a reality. Vin Featherstone, John Grimshaw, Ezra Firestone, Gabby Bernstein and Laura Gale, this could not have happened without you. And to everybody who gave me their time for interviews, case studies and advice, I am deeply grateful and so blessed to have you in my life. Thank you to the team at SmartMarketer, who moved mountains to get this book done. Finally, I am so thankful for my wonderful family, and my little pup Larry for seeing me through this process.

NOTES

4. THE STORY OF DIGITAL

1. https://www.statista.com/topics/871/online-shopping/
2. https://www.shopify.com/enterprise/global-ecommerce-statistics
3. http://www.pewinternet.org/2018/04/17/the-future-of-well-being-in-a-tech-saturated-world/
4. https://home.cern/news/news/computing/web30-reliving-history-and-rethinking-future
5. https://en.wikipedia.org/wiki/The_Innovator%27s_Dilemma
6. https://www.adweek.com/programmatic/u-s-digital-ad-spend-will-surpass-offline-in-2019/

5. A NEW WAY TO WORK

1. https://guilfordjournals.com/doi/10.1521/jscp.2018.37.10.751

11. A DAY IN THE LIFE OF A MEDIA BUYER

1. https://www.facebook.com/business/help/403110480493160?id=561906377587030

Made in the USA
Monee, IL
28 May 2020

32076479R00118